Instructor's Manual
to Accompany

Anthropology
A Perspective on the Human Condition

Robert H. Lavenda
St. Cloud State University

Emily A. Schultz
Macalester College

Mayfield Publishing Company
Mountain View, California
Toronto • London

ISBN: 1-55934-401-6

Manufactured in the United States of America
10 9 8 7 6 5 4 3 2 1

Mayfield Publishing Company
1280 Villa Street
Moutain View, California 94041

CONTENTS

INTRODUCTION

This manual is designed to be used with *Anthropology: A Perspective on the Human Condition,* by Emily A. Schultz and Robert H. Lavenda. It offers users of the text a set of pedagogical materials, including summaries of each chapter, lists of key terms, suggested readings, innovative "Arguing Anthropology" questions, information on ethnographic films, and ideas for stimulating class discussion. An extensive set of test questions is also included for each chapter.

The "Arguing Anthropology" questions in each chapter, which are also in the Study Guide for this text, are written to be provocative, to be argued, and to stimulate students to connect anthropology with their lives. Our hope is that students will form study groups for which these questions will be a focus of discussion. These same questions are in both the Instructor's Manual and the Study Guide.

This Instructor's Manual has an extensive selection of multiple-choice and essay questions for each chapter. We did not include any true-false questions because we don't feel that they work well with this text, given its position on interpretation. You should feel free to modify any of these questions to fit your particular needs. The essay questions may be used in two ways. They can be given conventionally—students do not see them until the exam begins—or they can be distributed a week before the exam as study questions, and then you can select which question or questions the students answer on the day of the exam. We have used the latter approach for several years, and have been pleased with the improvement in the quality of the answers. We would be pleased to hear from you regarding successful exam questions and testing strategies.

The information on ethnographic films and ideas for stimulating class discussions are designed to provide some hints for incorporating these techniques into the course. We would also draw your attention to the Sage Publications series, *Survival Skills for Scholars,* whose volumes on improving classroom teaching and tips for improving testing and grading make interesting reading even for the most experienced of us.

A NOTE ON ETHNOGRAPHIC FILMS

In our experience, it is difficult to give advice about the use of ethnographic film in the classroom. There is a remarkable, if bewildering, profusion of ethnographic films available now, and more are released all the time. Instructors have different interests and tastes, as well as varied financial resources and class time available to them. How film is used in the classroom is intensely personal. Films that some instructors find tremendously successful as teaching tools leave others cold, while probably each of us has a film or two that we use constantly but that no one else seems to value as much. As a result, we have chosen the following strategy. First, we are providing references to review, filmographies, and catalogs of several major ethnographic film collections so that instructors can find the films that will work best with their courses. Second, we have indicated a very small selection of films that are available about groups of people that are discussed at length in the text. The list is neither exhaustive nor exclusive; there are many more superb films that can be used. Third, over the last decade, PBS in the United States has shown a number of series that deal with anthropological topics, both physical and cultural, and some instructors may wish to consider using programs from those series. The Discovery Channel also shows films on anthropological topics. Many of these programs come from Granada TV's *Disappearing World* series.

Despite the visual literacy of present-day students, ethnographic films still work best when they are prepared for in advance or discussed carefully afterward. In a large class, it may be desirable (or necessary) to require a writing assignment for each film shown. These need not be elaborate: a single paragraph response to a question that requires attention to the film that is handed in at the end of the class may be sufficient. Instructors who are involved with a writing-across-the-curriculum program may wish to incorporate film reviews or responses into the journals or other writing assignments they employ.

Additionally, some ethnographic films come with study guides. In some cases, they are included in the film container. Other times, availability is noted in the film catalog or in the Heider catalog referenced below. It hardly needs adding that all films are products of their time—instructors should not expect them to exhibit a mid-1990s sensibility. To avoid unpleasant surprises, it is important to try to preview films or to read reviews before ordering. It may well be the case, however, that the visual data are so valuable in an older film that the instructor may want to use it anyway, while also spending some time with the class analyzing the narration or the visual semantics as evidence of perceptions of other societies that were characteristic of the time the film was made.

Topic	Film
Evolution	How Scientists Know About Human Evolution How Scientists Know About Punctuated Equilibria Stephen Jay Gould: This View of Life
Primates	Among the Wild Chimpanzees: A Life in the Trees
Archaeology	Other People's Garbage: A Lesson in Archaeology Seeking the First Americans The Making of Ancient Iron
Human Evolution	In Search of Human Origins (three episodes) Origins of Mankind; The Children of Eve Blades and Pressure Flaking
Prehistory	Iceman The Lost Tribe The Chaco Legacy Maya Lords of the Jungle Power, Prestige and Wealth Myths and the Moundbuilders Old Treasures from New China The Chinampas The Incas
Language	American Tongues Signs of the Apes, Songs of the Whales Colorless Green Ideas He Said, She Said An Evening with Deborah Tannen

People	Film
Trobriand Islanders	Trobriand Cricket The Trobriand Islanders of Papua New Guinea
Ju'/hoansi	N!ai, the Story of a !Kung Woman The Hunters at least 25 other films also available
Ashanti	Asante Market Women
Azande	Witchcraft Among the Azande
Nuer	The Nuer

2

Huichol	To Find Our Life: The Peyote Hunt of the Huichol Indians
	Huichol Sacred Pilgrimage to Wirikuta
Papua New Guinea	First Contact
	Joe Leahy's Neighbors
	Ongka's Big Moka
	The Lau of Malaita
	Dead Birds
Navajo	Dineh Nation
Yanomamo	A Man Called Bee: Studying the Yanomamo twenty other films by Napolean Chagnon also available
	Contact: The Yanomami Indians of Brazil
Yoruba	Yoruba Ritual
East African herders	Masai Women
	The Turkana
	Diary of a Maasai Village (five programs)
	The Women's Olamal

Resources for Anthropological Film

American Anthropologist publishes numerous film reviews in each issue. All films reviewed are also indexed in the annual index to the *American Anthropologist,* published with the December issue.

Films for Anthropological Teaching, Seventh Edition, 1983, by Karl Heider. American Anthropological Association, 1703 New Hampshire Ave., NW, Washington, D.C. 20009. $10.00 for members of the AAA, $15.00 for nonmembers. An especially important resource, the seventh edition of this guide contains descriptions of 1,575 films (twice as many as the sixth edition) used by anthropologists in teaching. It includes film titles, descriptions, bibliographies, prices and distributors, as well as geographical and topical listings of the films.

Films from D.E.R., 1982, and *D.E.R.: A New Generation of Film,* 1986, by Toby Alice Volkman. Documentary Educational Resources, 101 Morse Street, Watertown, MA 02172; (617) 926-0491; FAX, (617) 926-9519. $3.00 for 1982 catalog. D.E.R is a nonprofit organization established in 1971 to produce, distribute, and promote the use of ethnographic and documentary films. In the early 1970s, they concentrated on the !Kung San film project with John Marshall and the Yanomamo film project of Napolean Chagnon and Timothy Asch. They have since added films from many other parts of the world, including the films from the PBS *Odyssey* series. In the 1982 edition, they published an annotated catalog of the approximately 100 films in their collection. The annotations, and especially the essays about their film holdings for every geographic area, are themselves valuable teaching tools. In 1986, a supplement to the catalog was published detailing the 35 films that have recently been added to the collection. Since that time, regular updates have been issued. In 1983, D.E.R. published Toby Alice Volkman's 56-page study guide *N!ai: The Story of a !Kung Woman.*

Margaret Mead Film Festival, American Museum of Natural History, Central Park West at 79th Street, New York, NY 10024; (212) 873-1070. This four-day festival of ethnographic film in honor of Margaret Mead is approaching its fifteenth anniversary. The films screened each year represent some of the most interesting and innovative films in anthropology. The festival publishes an annual annotated brochure. A touring film exhibition from the festival, selected by Malcolm Arth, is available from the American Federation of Arts, 41 East 65th Street, New York, NY 10021.

Faces of Change Series, produced by the American Universities Field Staff in the 1970s. These are films that detail aspects of the lives of people in five places in the world: Kenya Boran, Afghanistan, the China Coast, Taiwan, and Bolivian Aymara. The films and excellent elaborate study guides are available from Documentary Educational Resources, 101 Morse Street, Watertown, MA 02172; (617) 926-0491; FAX, (617) 926-9519.

The following three university film and video centers have major collections of anthropological films and publish extensive annotated catalogs.

Indiana University
Audiovisual Center
Bloomington, IN 47405
Catalog title: *Catalog of Film and Video.* Listing of all anthropology films available on request.

The Pennsylviania State University
Audiovisual Services
Special Services Building
University Park, PA 16802
(814) 865-6314; or for scheduling only
(800) 826-0132
Catalog title: *Films: The Visualization of Anthropology*

University of California Extension
Media Center
2176 Shattuck Ave.
Berkeley, CA 94704
(415) 642-0462
Catalog title: *University of California Extension Media Center Film and Video Rental Catalog.* Issued every two years. Catalog of films for purchase also available.

The following two sources sell or rent a large number of anthropological films.

Filmakers Library
124 East 40th St.
New York, NY 10016
(212) 808-4980
(sale and rental; a large and interesting collection of ethnographic films)

Films Incorporated Video
5547 N. Ravenswood Ave.
Chicago, IL 60640
(800)343-4312
(sale only; many series holdings)

SUGGESTIONS FOR CLASS DISCUSSIONS

Small-group discussion has become an increasingly popular in-class learning technique in college courses. More and more students are being taught discussion skills, and many are coming to expect that small-group discussion will form part of each course they take. This may pose a challenge to instructors who are familiar with discussion in advanced seminars but are more accustomed to lecturing in introductory courses. In our experience, however, small-group discussions can be integrated into introductory-level anthropology classes without requiring massive restructuring of the syllabus.

1. Discussion need not take place every day. Students are satisfied with four or five days per term exclusively devoted to small-group discussion.

2. Discussion days can easily be integrated into your regular syllabus by assigning special readings that relate to the topic currently being covered in the textbook and lectures. If, in additon to this textbook, your students are using a volume of collected essays (such as Podolefsky and Brown's *Applying Anthropology* or Spradley and McCurdy's *Conformity and Conflict*), you will find a good selection of apt articles to choose from. You may want to assign two or three articles on the same topic and use all of them as resources for a discussion devoted to that topic.

3. Discussions work better if they are focused. One way to provide focus is to provide your students at the beginning of class with a quotation (preferably a somewhat provocative quotation) taken from one of the assigned readings or elsewhere, that bears directly on the discussion topic. Then ask the students to assess the material they have read in light of this quotation. Another, similar technique is to hand out copies of a short newspaper article or some other short text that addresses the day's topic and use that as the focus for discussion.

4. Students are more likely to engage in productive discussion if they are given time to think before they speak. If you present them with a quotation or a text, it is helpful to allow them five minutes or so to reflect and to jot down possible responses to the quotation or text. After this, you can break the class into groups of four to six students, and the small-group discussions can begin.

5. Students may focus better on the task at hand if they have a simple format to follow. For example, they can choose one person to be the Recording Secretary, who will record the various points made by each member as the discussion proceeds. The Recording Secretary might also be responsible for making sure that each member of the group is given an opportunity to speak. You can move from group to group to listen in and to respond to any questions students might have. It is easy to tell when students have run out of things to discuss: the noise level in the room increases and one overhears comments about last night's football game or plans for the weekend. Twenty minutes of discussion is probably enough for most topics.

6. After the small groups have been discussing for 20 minutes or so, and if they seem to have fairly thoroughly explored the assigned topic, the class can be reunited for the remainder of the class period. Each group can be called on in turn to share the results of their discussion with the rest of the class. You can write key points on the board, and the final result can then be examined by the entire class for common themes.

7. Students need to see that you value their efforts enough to make part of their grade dependent on participation in discussions. If the Recording Secretary of each discussion group writes the names of all group members on the notes s/he takes during discussion, and the instructor collects these notes at the end of class, points that will count for their final grade can be awarded to participants, and if one must be present for the discussion to earn those points, students will take discussions seriously.

CHAPTER 1

THE ANTHROPOLOGICAL PERSPECTIVE

Outline

WHAT IS ANTHROPOLOGY?

THE CONCEPT OF CULTURE

THE CROSS-DISCIPLINARY DISCIPLINE

Physical Anthropology (Biological Anthropology)
Cultural Anthropology
Anthropological Linguistics
Archaeology
Applied Anthropology

ANTHROPOLOGY, SCIENCE, AND STORYTELLING

SOME KEY SCIENTIFIC CONCEPTS

Assumptions
Evidence
Hypotheses
Testability
Theories
Objectivity

USES OF ANTHROPOLOGY

Key Terms

anthropology
holistic
comparative
evolutionary
culture
biocultural organisms
physical anthropology
   (biological
   anthropology)
races
racism

biological anthropologists
primatologists
paleonanthropologists
cultural anthropology
language
anthropological
   linguistics
fieldwork
informants
ethnography
ethnology

archaeology
applied anthropology
myths
science
assumptions
evidence
hypotheses
testability
scientific theory
objectivity

Arguing Anthropology

1. What sets science apart from other kinds of storytelling?

2. Why might human diversity be threatening in some circumstances?

Multiple Choice Questions

1. In the textbook, anthropology is defined as the study of
* a.   human nature, human society, and the human past.
  b.   the remains of earlier societies and peoples.
  c.   the ways of life of contemporary peoples.
  d.   the physical and mental capacities of human beings.

2. Holism in anthropology is defined in the text as
  a.   trying to study everything possible about a people during the course of a research trip.
* b.   integrating what is known about human beings and their activities at an inclusive level.
  c.   studying human biology and culture at the same time.
  d.   fitting together economics, political science, religious studies, and biology.

3. To say that anthropology is comparative means that
  a.   each anthropologist studies many different cultures during his or her career.
* b.   anthropological generalizations must draw on evidence from many cultures.
  c.   anthropologists use data from many different academic fields of study when they do their research.
  d.   there is no one way for the anthropologist to do research.

4. Which of the following is NOT an element of the anthropological perspective?
  a.   holism
  b.   comparison
  c.   an evolutionary approach
* d.   learning dependent

5. A study that examines how economics, politics, religion, and kinship shape one another in a specific society would be
  a.   detailed.
  b.   cultural.
* c.   holistic.
  d.   comparative.

6. An anthropologist studying a social group observes that people shake hands when greeting one another and concludes that handshaking is universal among human beings. This study is faulty because the anthropologist has not been
a.   holistic.
b.   evolutionary.
c.   ethnocentric.
* d.   comparative.

7. According to the text, evolution may be understood broadly as
a.   attributes and behaviors that are passed on by the genes.
b.   beliefs and behaviors that are passed on by teaching and learning.
* c.   change over time.
d.   transformations of species over time.

8. According to the text, culture consists of
* a.   sets of learned behaviors and ideas that human beings acquire as members of society.
b.   those elements of the human experience that require education and good taste: art, music, dance.
c.   sets of innate instincts that enable human beings to function in a complex world.
d.   those sets of behaviors and ideas that enable human beings to appreciate differences between one society and another.

9. According to the text, the concept that is defined as sets of learned behavior and ideas that human beings acquire as members of society is the concept of
a.   race.
* b.   culture.
c.   instinct.
d.   biocultural inheritance.

10. To claim that members of a particular social group do not typically eat insects because they have learned to label insects as inedible is to use an explanation based on
* a.   culture.
b.   biology.
c.   ethnocentrism.
d.   genetic programming.

11. To emphasize that human beings are biocultural organisms means that
   a.   human biology and culture both contribute to human behavior.
   b.   human biology makes culture possible and human culture makes
         human biological survival possible.
   c.   instinct must be recognized as an important part of any explanation of
         human behavior.
* d.   both a and b are true.

12. When anthropologists distinguish between Culture and cultures, they are
    distinguishing between _____ and _____
   a.   different traditions of learned behavior; the ability to learn and to create
         sets of behaviors and ideas.
* b.   a defining attribute of human beings; specific local traditions.
   c.   the fine arts; local traditions.
   d.   the innate instincts that set human beings apart from other organisms;
         the ways in which these instincts work in specific places.

13. To say that anthropology is a field-based discipline means that
   a.   information about particular cultures comes through direct contact with
         them.
   b.   all anthropology is based on experience with other ways of life.
   c.   the experience of being in the field is central to modern anthropology.
* d.   all of the above are true.

14. The branch of anthropology that is concerned with discovering what makes
    human beings different from other living organisms and what human beings
    share with other members of the animal kingdom is called
   a.   applied anthropology.
   b.   archaeology.
* c.   biological anthropology.
   d.   cultural anthropology.

15. Physical anthropologists are interested in
   a.   the material remains of the human past.
* b.   human beings as biological organisms.
   c.   present-day social arrangements in human groups.
   d.   human symbolic communication.

16. Which of the following is NOT a major subfield of anthropology?
   a.   archaeology
   b.   cultural anthropology
   c.   biological anthropology
* d.   physiological anthropology

17. Unambiguous categories based on distinct sets of biological attributes are called
* a.   races.
  b.   populations.
  c.   cultures.
  d.   criteria.

18. By the early twentieth century, some anthropologists and biologists concluded that the concept of "race" was
  a.   justified by the increasingly scientific biological research on human beings.
* b.   a cultural label invented by human beings to sort people into groups.
  c.   a political liability, although the evidence was increasingly strong in its favor.
  d.   a label that recognized important intellectual and biological differences among groups.

19. The people of society X believe that the people of society Y are inherently inferior to them biologically, and prevent them from gaining access to a high level of education and other resources. According to the text, this is an example of
* a.   racism.
  b.   ethnocentrism.
  c.   labeling.
  d.   holism.

20. A contemporary biological anthropologist is likely to study
  a.   the relationship of nutrition and physical development.
  b.   non-human primates.
  c.   human origins.
* d.   any of the above

21. Paleoanthropologists study
  a.   modern apes.
  b.   human variation.
* c.   fossilized bones and teeth.
  d.   nutrition and physical development.

22. A contemporary cultural anthropologist is likely to study
  a.   political institutions in a village in another country.
  b.   kinship systems in an urban setting.
  c.   patterns of material life in his or her own society.
* d.   any of the above

23. The system of arbitrary vocal symbols we use to encode out experience of the world and of one another is called
   a.   culture.
* b.   language.
   c.   linguistics.
   d.   symbolism.

24. An extended period of close involvement by anthropologists with the people whose life is of interest to them is called
* a.   fieldwork.
   b.   surveying.
   c.   interviewing.
   d.   information gathering.

25. To cultural anthropologists, informants are people who
   a.   are willing to share secrets about the lives of others in their community.
   b.   read the books and articles that cultural anthropologists write.
* c.   share information about their culture and language with anthropologists.
   d.   serve as research subjects.

26. An anthropologist is sitting in the town square in a Bolivian village watching a group of women who are chatting. One wanders over and asks the anthropologist if she would like to join them in shopping for thread for their looms and then helping to string the looms. She agrees, and they go off together. This form of research is called
* a.   participant-observation.
   b.   working with informants.
   c.   cultural sharing.
   d.   reciprocal research.

27. The anthropological research methodology called participant-observation is characterized by
   a.   long-term intensive interviewing of informants.
   b.   spending extended periods of time both watching and recording behavior, especially in public places.
* c.   both getting involved in social activities and watching those activities.
   d.   becoming a member of the society being studied.

28. A description of a particular culture is called an
    a.   ethnohistory.
* b.   ethnography.
    c.   ethnology.
    d.   ethnographer.

29. A comparative study of many cultures is called an
    a.   ethnohistory.
    b.   ethnography.
* c.   ethnology.
    d.   ethnographer.

30. The major specialty within anthropology that involves the analysis of the material remains of the human past is
    a.   applied anthropology.
* b.   archaeology.
    c.   biological anthropology.
    d.   cultural anthropology.

31. The major specialty within anthropology that uses information gathered from the other subfields in an effort to solve practical cross-cultural problems is
* a.   applied anthropology.
    b.   archaeology.
    c.   biological anthropology.
    d.   cultural anthropology.

32. A narrative account of how things got to be the way they are is a
    a.   scientific theory.
    b.   hypothesis.
    c.   myth.
* d.   a and c

33. For anthropologists, stories whose truth seems self-evident because the stories integrate personal experiences with wider assumptions about the world are called
* a.   myths.
    b.   scientific theories.
    c.   folktales.
    d.   hypotheses.

34. Explanations of the world that are explicitly open-ended and self-correcting are called
   a.   myths.
* b.   scientific theories.
   c.   folktales.
   d.   hypotheses.

35. What sets science apart from other forms of explanation is that science is
* a.   empirical, open-ended, and self-correcting.
   b.   experimental and concerned with facts.
   c.   provable and valid.
   d.   a form of language that creates verifiable propositions.

36. Basic understandings about the way the world works that are never questioned are called
* a.   assumptions.
   b.   evidence.
   c.   hypotheses.
   d.   theories.

37. When university students in the United States walk into a classroom, they expect that the class will have an instructor who will assess their work and give them grades. These expectations are called
* a.   assumptions.
   b.   hypotheses.
   c.   theories.
   d.   evidentiary.

38. What observers can see when they observe a particular part of the world with great care is called
   a.   assumptions.
* b.   evidence.
   c.   hypotheses.
   d.   theories.

39. Statements that assert a particular connection between fact and interpretations are called
   a.   assumptions.
   b.   evidence.
* c.   hypotheses.
   d.   theories.

40. When university students in the United States walk into a classroom on the first day, they observe that there is a person standing in the front of the classroom with a folder open on a podium and a stack of papers on the desk. Based on their experience, they decide that this must be the instructor. Decisions of this kind are called
   a.   assumptions.
   b.   evidence.
 * c.   hypotheses.
   d.   theories.

41. The capacity of scientific hypotheses to be matched against nature to see whether the hypotheses are confirmed or refuted is called
 * a.   testability.
   b.   objectivity.
   c.   theory building.
   d.   evidence.

42. When university students in the United States walk into a classroom on the first day, they observe that there is a person standing in the front of the classroom with a folder open on a podium and a stack of papers on the desk. Based on their experience, they decide that this must be the instructor. One student approaches the person and asks, "Are you the instructor?" The student's question is an example of
   a.   theory building.
   b.   an assumption.
 * c.   testability.
   d.   hypothesis formation.

43. If a hypothesis cannot be tested, it
   a.   can be used as an assumption.
   b.   is false.
   c.   can be used for evidence of other hypotheses.
 * d.   cannot be considered scientific.

44. A series of testable hypotheses that are linked in a coherent manner in order to explain a body of material evidence is called
   a.   a set of assumptions.
   b.   verifiable hypotheses.
 * c.   a scientific theory.
   d.   an objective meaning structure.

15

45. A scientific theory
  a.   is the result of studying data and testing hypotheses.
  b.   accounts for a wide range of material evidence.
  c.   remains open to testing and possible falsification.
* d.   all of the above

46. The separation of observation and reporting from the researcher's wishes refers to
  a.   assumptions.
  b.   hypothesis building.
* c.   objectivity.
  d.   testability.

47. The most powerful scientific theories are those
  a.   based on a series of powerful assumptions about the world.
* b.   whose hypotheses have been tested often and have never been falsified.
  c.   most closely tied to the nature of the reality they describe.
  d.   that combine both material and inferred evidence in new and effective ways.

49. Since total objectivity is impossible, should people choose the theories they like best?
  a.   Yes, since one theory is as good as any other.
  b.   Yes, since all theories are true to some degree.
  c.   No, since scientists will eventually discover the truth, even if they do not know it now.
* d.   No, since some theories better account for more important data than do others.

50. In a world in which people from different cultural backgrounds come into contact with one another for extended periods, anthropology offers a
  a.   solution to cultural misunderstandings.
* b.   means of learning to cope with cultural differences.
  c.   way of determining which cultural background is better under the circumstances.
  d.   set of techniques for removing cultural barriers.

Essay Questions

51. Choose one of the five subdisciplines in anthropology and explain what is distinctive about its approach to the human condition.

52. How might a college undergraduate benefit from taking a course in cultural anthropology?

53. Write a short definition of anthropology and describe its connection to the social sciences, the natural sciences, and the humanities.

54. What does it mean when anthropologists claim that their discipline is holistic, comparative, and evolutionary?

55. Discuss the nature of objectivity in anthropology. How is it connected with the other aspects of a scientific approach?

56. Why are scientific theories taken seriously by scientists?

57. In the text, the authors discuss how scientists might approach a hypothesis that claimed that aliens from another planet had "planted" fossils of supposed human ancestors in the earth about 10,000 years ago. How would scientists go about testing that hypothesis?

CHAPTER 2

EVOLUTION

Outline

EVOLUTIONARY THEORY

MATERIAL EVIDENCE FOR EVOLUTION

PRE-DARWINIAN VIEWS OF THE NATURAL WORLD

Essentialism
The Great Chain of Being
Natural Theology: Catastrophism and Uniformitarianism
Transformational Evolution

THE THEORY OF NATURAL SELECTION

UNLOCKING THE SECRETS OF HEREDITY

Mendel
"There Is No 'Race Memory' in Biology, Only in Books"

GENOTYPE, PHENOTYPE, AND THE NORM OF REACTION

WHAT DOES EVOLUTION MEAN?

Key Terms

evolutionary theory
evolution
essentialism
Great Chain of Being
taxonomy
species
genus
catastrophism
uniformitarianism
transformational
   evolution
common descent
natural selection
variational evolution

fitness
pangenesis
Mendelian inheritance
principle of segregation
principle of independent
   assortment
genetics
homozygous
heterozygous
genes
alleles
chromosomes
mitosis

meiosis
linkage
crossing over
discontinuous variation
polygeny
continuous variation
pleiotropy
mutation
DNA
locus
genotype
phenotype
norm of reaction

Arguing Anthropology

1. Even though the Darwinian concept of natural selection does not require the idea of "the survival of the fittest," why is the idea so popular?

2. Consider the following statement. "The only certainty about the future of our species is that it is limited. Of all the species that have ever existed 99.999% are extinct." What might be the implications for human beings and for human societies?

Multiple Choice Questions

1. Evolutionary theory claims that
   a. living organisms can change over time and give rise to new kinds of living organisms.
   b. all organisms ultimately share a common ancestry.
   c. information about biological variation in different organisms provides information valuable to the study of human variation.
 * d. all of the above are true.

2. According to the text, the fossil record provides for the theory of evolution information about
 * a. remains of ancient life forms that were different from present day life forms.
   b. unchanging life forms over extended periods of time.
   c. the ways in which life forms were created and how they have stayed the same from their moment of origin to the present.
   d. a and b

3. The study of living organisms has been important to evolutionary theory because
   a. it is possible to determine the patterns of evolution from the present form of a specific species.
   b. it provides material evidence of change over space
   c. geographic patterns of distribution of related species of organisms can demonstrate patterns of change
 * d. b and c

4. The philosophical approach that sees objects as possessed of ideal forms that define their kind is known as
   a. uniformitarianism.
   b. idealism.
 * c. essentialism.
   d. organicism.

5. A single hierarchy of all organisms, each differing slightly from the ones above it and below it, was known as
* a.   the Great Chain of Being.
  b.   binomial nomenclature.
  c.   essentialism.
  d.   catastrophism.

6. The "father of modern biological classification" is the title often given to
  a.   Ernst Mayr.
* b.   Carolus Linnaeus.
  c.   Charles Darwin.
  d.   Lamarck.

6. A system of biological classification is called a
  a.   great chain of being.
  b.   genus.
* c.   taxonomy.
  d.   plenitude.

7. A taxonomy is
* a.   a system of classification.
  b.   another term for species.
  c.   a form of essentialism.
  d.   a way of ranking different species from lowest to highest.

8. The term catastrophism refers to the idea that
* a.   natural disasters are responsible for the extinction of species.
  b.   there was a ladder of species ordered from lowest to highest.
  c.   the same processes that worked in the past continue to work equally in the present.
  d.   species emerge by eliminating other species.

9. The idea that natural disasters are responsible for the extinction of species is known as
* a.   catastrophism.
  b.   essentialism.
  c.   gradualism.
  d.   uniformitarianism.

10. The idea that the same gradual geologic processes that change the earth's surface today were also at work in the past is known as
    a.   catastrophism.
    b.   essentialism.
    c.   gradualism.
*   d.   uniformitarianism.

11. The term uniformitarianism refers to the idea that
    a.   natural disasters are responsible for the extinction of species.
    b.   there was a ladder of species ordered from lowest to highest.
*   c.   the same processes that worked in the past continue to work equally in the present.
    d.   species emerge by eliminating other species.

12. Neither catastrophism nor uniformitarianism was very good at explaining the
    a.   workings of natural law.
    b.   diversity of species.
*   c.   origins of living things.
    d.   process of extinction.

13. The idea that fossil species were the ancestors of living species was suggested by
*   a.   Lamarck.
    b.   Darwin.
    c.   Cuvier.
    d.   Lyell.

14. The idea of the inheritance of acquired characters holds that
*   a.   the physical result of the use or disuse of organs could be passed from one generation to the next.
    b.   the environment does not allow for certain accidentally acquired characteristics to be passed from one generation to the next.
    c.   as a species adapts to an environment, changes in gene frequency are passed to the next generation.
    d.   only those characteristics that are acquired may be inherited.

15. The Panda's elongated wristbone or "thumb" would be explained by Lamarck's theory in which of the following ways?

* a.   Some pandas acquired "thumbs" through strenuous activity and then produced offspring with the same characteristic.

   b.   Some pandas had "thumbs" of different lengths, and in a new environment, those with longer "thumbs" were better able to survive and produce offspring.

   c.   Some pandas acquired "thumbs" through strenuous activity and were better able to survive.

   d.   Some pandas had longer "thumbs" and were able to produce offspring.

16. The Panda's elongated wristbone or "thumb" would be explained by Darwin's theory in which of the following ways?

   a.   Some pandas acquired "thumbs" through strenuous activity and then produced offspring with the same characteristic.

* b.   Some pandas had "thumbs" of different lengths, and in a new environment, those with longer "thumbs" were better able to survive and produce offspring.

   c.   Some pandas acquired "thumbs" through strenuous activity and were better able to survive.

   d.   Some pandas had longer "thumbs" and were able to produce offspring.

17. The theory of common descent holds that

   a.   all species are related to each other.

* b.   similar species are descended from a common ancestor.

   c.   similar species are able to interbreed.

   d.   all species reproduce in a similar ("common") way.

18. Darwin's innovation in defining the species was to emphasize

   a.   what members of a species have in common.

   b.   the connections of species to other species.

* c.   how individual members of a species differ.

   d.   the survival potential of the species.

19. Which of the following is NOT an element of Darwin's theory of evolution by natural selection?

* a.   crossing-over.

   b.   natural selection.

   c.   struggle for existence.

   d.   variation.

20. In Darwinian terms, who are the fit?
a. 　　　the most powerful.
b. 　　　those who survive.
c. 　　　those who reproduce.
d. 　　　those who cooperate with others.

21. Pangenesis is a theory of inheritance that holds that an organism's physical traits are
a. 　　　passed from the grandparental generation, skipping the parental generation.
b. 　　　passed from one generation to the next in the form of particles.
c. 　　　part of the human family and are inherited from the ancient human past.
d. 　　　both b and c

22. When peas with red flowers are crossed with peas with white flowers, in the second generation what will be the ratio of one trait to the other?
a. 　　　1:4
b. 　　　1:3
c. 　　　1:2
d. 　　　1:1

23. Mendelian inheritance is
a. 　　　blending, multiple-particle.
b. 　　　blending, single-particle.
c. 　　　nonblending, multi-particle.
d. 　　　nonblending, single-particle.

24. Those genetic characteristics that are expressed in an organism are said to be
a. 　　　dominant.
b. 　　　genetic.
c. 　　　homozygous.
d. 　　　recessive.

25. Those genetic characteristics that are not expressed in an organism are said to be
a. 　　　dominant.
b. 　　　genetic.
c. 　　　homozygous.
d. 　　　recessive.

26. In modern terms, Mendel's principle of segregation holds that
   a.   plants are able to pass genetic information from one generation to the other without sexual reproduction.
   b.   there are two chromosomes for each physical trait.
* c.   an individual receives one chromosome of each pair of chromosomes from each parent.
   d   each pair of chromosomes is capable of separating into two separate strands.

27. In modern terms, Mendel's principle of independent assortment holds that
   a.   each pair of chromosomes separates independently of every other pair of chromosomes when sex cells are formed.
   b.   chromosomes sort themselves according to a genetically inherited sequence that is independent of any other pattern.
   c.   the set of chromosomes that come together in any individual is random.
* d.   both a and c are true.

28. A fertilized egg that has received a different form of a specific gene from each parent is called
   a.   homozygous.
* b.   heterozygous.
   c.   allele-identical.
   d.   chromosomal.

29. homozygous:heterozygous::
* a.   same:different
   b.   fertilized:unfertilized
   c.   genetics:heredity
   d.   genes:alleles

30. Every pair of chromosomes in human beings is homologous except for
   a.   the X and Y chromosomes.
   b.   the chromosomes that are responsible for aging.
   c.   the sex chromosomes.
* d.   both a and c

31. A person who is homozygous for the X chromosome is
   a.   male.
* b.   female.
   c.   gendered.
   d.   there is not enough information to say.

32. A person who is heterozygous for the X and Y chromosomes is
a.   male.
b.   female.
c.   gendered.
d.   There is not enough information to say.

33. In genetics, the phenomenon known as crossing over occurs when
a.   two chromosomes are passed on together.
b.   part of a chromosome breaks off and reattaches itself to a different
       chromosome.
c.   two genes near each other on the same chromosome have an effect on a
       trait.
d.   there is discontinuous variation.

34. A situation in which one dominant or two identical recessive characteristics
    determine a single trait is called
a.   continuous variation.
b.   discontinuous variation.
c.   linkage.
d.   polygeny.

35. polygeny/pleiotropy:
a.   homozygous/heterozygous
b.   one/many
c.   many and one/one and many
d.   blood type/skin color

36. The situation in which two or more genes are responsible for producing a
    single trait is called
a.   linkage.
b.   polygeny.
c.   polyzygous.
d.   pleiotropy.

37. The situation in which one gene may affect more than one trait is called
a.   linkage.
b.   polygeny.
c.   polyzygous.
d.   pleiotropy.

38. That the allele that gives human red blood cells increased resistance to malarial parasites also reduces the amount of oxygen those cells can carry demonstrates
   a.   genotype.
   b.   phenotype.
   c.   polygeny.
* d.   pleiotropy.

39. The difference between theories of unchanging inheritance and theories of modifiable inheritance
   a.   is in the connection between the adaptive needs of an organism and the information in the sex cells.
   b.   is in the importance of preexisting variation within the species.
   c.   is the nature of mutation.
* d.   is all of the above.

40. Natural selection acts on
   a.   mutations.
   b.   the needs of a species.
* c.   randomly produced variation.
   d.   the sex cells.

41. Chromosomes are made up of strands of
* a.   deoxyribonucleic acid.
   b.   guanine.
   c.   cytosine.
   d.   ribonucleic acid.

42. The biochemical structure for transmitting genetic information regarding the construction and development of a particular organism is
   a.   adenine.
* b.   DNA.
   c.   MFT.
   d.   RNA.

43. guanine:cytosine::
   a.   adenine:riboflavin
* b.   thymine:adenine
   c.   DNA:RNA
   d.   Laurel:Hardy

44. genotype:phenotype::
a.   structure:function
b.   instructions:outcome
c.   plan:planner
d.   results:genes

45. Mutations that neither help nor harm an organism are called
a.   allele mutations.
b.   neutral mutations.
c.   regulatory mutations.
d.   value-free mutations.

46. Which of the following does NOT alter the structure of the DNA code?
a.   chemicals
b.   heat
c.   radiation
d.   weight

47. The notion that something experienced by individuals in one generation can
be genetically transmitted to their offspring and become a permanent part of
their genetic heritage is referred to in the text as
a.   genetic learning.
b.   natural selection.
c.   race memory.
d.   selection pressure.

48. The realization of a _____ is called the _____.
a.   genotype; phenotype
b.   phenotype; genotype
c.   phenotype; norm of reaction
d.   genotype; norm of reaction

49. The total set of information carried in an organism's genes is called the
a.   genotype.
b.   infrabar.
c.   phenotype.
d.   ultrabar.

50. The observable, measurable characteristics that are based on the genetic inheritance of an organism are called the
    a.   genotype.
    b.   infrabar.
* c.   phenotype.
    d.   ultrabar.

51. _____ genotypes may produce _____ phenotypes.
    a.   Different; different
    b.   Different; the same
    c.   The same; different
* d.   all of the above

52. The norm of reaction specifies
* a.   how, given a specific genotype, a developing organism will respond to various environments.
    b.   how, given a specific environment, a given genotype will be transformed.
    c.   the normal way in which a genotype produces its phenotype.
    d.   the way in which, under a specific environment, a phenotype reacts to its genotype.

53. At 6000 calories a day, a person with genotype X will weigh 285 lbs with much energy and high cholesterol levels. At 3500 calories a day, the person will weigh 200 lbs and have much energy and slightly elevated cholesterol levels. At 1800 calories a day, the person will weigh 175 lbs and have little energy and low cholesterol levels. These are examples of that genotype's
    a.   adaptive capacities.
    b.   environment.
* c.   norm of reaction.
    d.   This has nothing to do with the genotype.

54. The way in which genotype and environment interact to produce a phenotype is measured by the
    a.   overall size of the organism.
    b.   phenotypic index.
* c.   norm of reaction.
    d.   principle of independent assortment.

55. What is the likely future of a given species?
* a.   extinction
  b.   transformation via evolution into another species
  c.   stability
  d.   It depends on its genetic makeup.

Essay Questions

56. Discuss the material evidence for evolution.

57. Compare and contrast the positions of catastrophism and uniformitarianism.

58. How would a scholar following the work of Lamarck explain the elephant's trunk? How would a Darwinian?

59. What are the key elements of Darwin's approach to evolution? Why are they important?

60. What is the significance of variation in evolution by natural selection? Be sure to illustrate your answer with specific examples.

61. Is there such a thing as "absolute fitness"? Why or why not?

62. What are some of the ways in which sexual reproduction maintains or increases variation? Why is this significant?

63. What are polygeny and pleiotropy? Why are they important?

64. What is the significance for human beings of the facts that different genotypes can produce the same phenotypes in some environments and that the same genotype can produce different phenotypes in different environments?

CHAPTER 3

MICROEVOLUTION AND MACROEVOLUTION: HUMAN EVOLUTION IN THE SHORT AND LONG TERM

Outline

MICROEVOLUTION

The Modern Evolutionary Synthesis and Its Legacy
The Four Evolutionary Forces
Microevolution and Patterns of Human Variation
Human Variation
Sociobiology
The Importance of Phenotypes
The Evolution of Culture
Group Selection

MACROEVOLUTION

THE FUTURE OF HUMAN EVOLUTION

Key Terms

microevolution	adaptation	kin selection
macroevolution	plasticity	parental investment
species	acclimatization	ethology
gene pool	developmental	indirect bias
gene frequencies	acclimatization	group selection
population genetics	Bergmann's rule	anagenesis
mitochondrial DNA	Allen's rule	phyletic gradualism
natural selection	allometry	cladogenesis
mutation	sociobiology	punctuated equilibrium
gene flow	altruism	species selection
genetic drift	inclusive fitness	

Arguing Anthropology

1. "Physical life and a meaningful life usually, but not always, go together." In your opinion, at what point do they stop going together?

2. As genetic research advances, it becomes increasingly possible for human beings to intervene in the genetic processes that affect them (some examples are the human genome project, assisted reproduction, pre-natal genetic testing, and gene cloning). To what degree *should* human beings intervene in the genetic processes that affect them?

Multiple Choice

1. The field of study that concentrates on short-term evolutionary changes that occur within a given species over a relatively few generations is called
   a.   macroevolution.
 * b.   microevolution.
   d.   modern synthesis.
   c.   natural selection.

2. The field of study that concentrates on long-term evolutionary changes that lead to new species and their diversification over a relatively long period of time is called
 * a.   macroevolution.
   b.   microevolution.
   d.   modern synthesis.
   c.   natural selection.

3. ecological time/geological time:
   a.   macroevolution/microevolution
 * b.   microevolution/macroevolution
   c.   origins/development
   d.   both b and c

4. A reproductive community of populations that occupies a specific niche is a
   a.   breeding group.
   b.   genus.
   c.   population.
 * d.   species.

5. A species
   a.   is a reproductive community.
   b.   is reproductively isolated.
   c.   occupies a specific niche.
 * d.   all of the above

6. All of the genes in the bodies of all members of a given species or
    population make up a
* a.   gene pool.
   b.   genotype.
   c.   gene frequency.
   d.   gene flow.

7. The field that focuses on the study of short-term evolutionary change in a
    given species is known as
   a.   genetics.
   b.   macrogenetics.
   c.   microgenetics.
* d.   population genetics.

8. The human genome is
   a.   the sum of all human phenotypic variation.
   b.   the gene frequencies of a given human population.
* c.   the sum total of human genetic information.
   d.   the study of human population genetics.

9. The largest component of overall human genetic diversity comes from
    differences that exist between
* a.   individuals from the same tribe or nationality.
   b.   nationalities.
   c.   human "races."
   d.   none of the above

10. A "pure" race, in biological terms, would be
   a.   a population that has interbred for at least 12 generations.
* b.   homozygous at every gene locus.
   c.   clearly distinguishable from all other races.
   d.   able to interbreed only with related races.

11. The genes that are carried outside the cell nucleus are called
   a.   acellular DNA.
   b.   cytoplasm.
* c.   mitochondrial DNA.
   d.   transfer RNA.

12. According to the text, the so-called black, red, yellow, and white "races" of human beings are based on
   a.   scientific observation of genetic differences among many different populations.
   b.   genotypically based behavioral differences on three major dimensions.
   c.   a human need to discriminate.
* d.   cultural elaboration of a few phenotypically based differences.

13. Which of the following is NOT one of the four evolutionary forces?
   a.   gene flow
   b.   genetic drift
   c.   mutation
* d.   plasticity

14. Gene frequencies may be altered if a given population begins to interbreed with another population of the same species. This is known as
* a.   gene flow.
   b.   genetic drift.
   c.   mutation.
   d.   natural selection.

15. Random changes in gene frequencies from one generation to the next due to a sudden reduction in population size resulting in the loss of particular alleles is known as
   a.   gene flow.
* b.   genetic drift.
   c.   mutation.
   d.   natural selection.

16. Which of the following is an example of genetic drift?
   a.   the bottleneck effect
   b.   the founder effect
   c.   the mutation effect
* d.   both a and b

17. Assume that in a small population, 15% of the people are blue-eyed and have brown hair. Assume further that within this population, there is an adventurous group that wishes to explore the region and settle down in new territory. Of this adventurous group, 87% are blue-eyed and have brown hair. When they leave, the gene frequencies in the remaining population will change for blue-eyes and brown hair in the next generation. This is an example of
   a.   gene flow.
* b.   genetic drift.
   c.   mutation.
   d.   natural selection.

18. A well-known example of a balanced polymorphism is
   a.   acclimatization response.
   b.   body shape in cold climates.
   c.   red hair color.
* d.   sickle-cell anemia.

19. A situation in which the heterozygous genotype is fitter than either of the homozygous genotypes is called
* a.   a balanced polymorphism.
   b.   Bregmann's Rule.
   c.   hemoglobin A.
   d.   a natural selection adjustment.

20. The example of the sickle-cell genotype illustrates
   a.   balanced polymorphism.
   b.   how cultural practices can affect biological selection pressures.
   c.   natural selection in action.
* d.   all of the above

21. The mutual shaping of organisms and their environments is known as
   a.   acclimatization.
* b.   adaptation.
   c.   plasticity.
   d.   pleiotropy.

22. When human beings move into an area that seems too cold for them, they can wear clothing, build shelters, or cluster around a fire. These activities can be called
* a.   adaptation.
   b.   environmental stress.
   c.   plasticity.
   d.   pleiotropy.

23. Which of the following is an example of acclimatization?
    a.   shivering.
*   b.   increased lung capacity in people raised at high altitudes.
    c.   increased male baldness in northern climates.
    d.   a and b

24. Which of the following body size and shape combinations loses heat best?
    a.   larger and more compact
*   b.   larger and more linear
    c.   smaller and more compact
    d.   smaller and more linear

25. Allen's Rule holds that animals in cold climates should have
*   a.   short, stout limbs.
    b.   short, thin limbs.
    c.   long, stout limbs.
    d.   long, thin limbs.

26. The rule that relates body size and shape to heat loss is
    a.   Allen's.
*   b.   Bergmann's.
    c.   Darwin's.
    d.   Lewin's.

27. The rule that relates limb size and shape to heat conservation is
*   a.   Allen's.
    b.   Bergmann's.
    c.   Darwin's.
    d.   Lewin's.

28. The rate at which different body parts grow in relation to one another is
    called
    a.   acclimatization.
    b.   allelometry.
*   c.   allometry.
    d.   clinal variation.

29. When variations in skin color of indigenous populations of the world are plotted on a map,
  a.   The populations with the lightest pigmentation live furthest from the equator.
  b.   The populations with the darkest pigmentation live closest to the equator.
  c.   skin color is randomly distributed throughout the world.
* d.   Both a and b are true.

30. The distribution of skin pigmentation from the poles to the equator forms a
* a.   cline.
  b.   chwartz.
  c.   goodmin.
  d.   koan.

31. Which of the following might be a selective advantage for dark skin in tropical human populations?
  a.   protection from early skin cancer
  b.   protection from infant dehydration due to sunburn
  c.   protection from sweating due to dehydration
* d.   both a and b

32. A hypothesis to explain the loss of skin pigmentation in higher latitudes is that less pigmentation is a defense against
  a.   too much vitamin D produced by the melanin in dark skin given the sunlight conditions.
* b.   cold injury.
  c.   skin cancer.
  d.   all of the above

33. Which of the following is a reason why scores on IQ tests do not demonstrate racial differences in intelligence?
  a.   the assumption that traits essential to racial identity are discrete and nonoverlapping is false.
  b.   differences between group scores on IQ tests may be due to cultural knowledge rather than intelligence.
  c.   social class and educational background are more accurate predictors of IQ scores.
* d.   All of the above are true.

34. Much recent research has demonstrated that IQ scores are
a.   based on the test-taker's genotype.
b.   determined about 60 percent by genes and about 40 percent by the environment.
c.   due to random factors such as temperature, noise, or mood, in the test-taking situation.
* d.   shaped by a range of environmental factors.

35. Recent research cited in the text shows that when African-Americans and European-Americans are matched in terms of social class and educational background, the differences in average IQ scores
a.   do not change.
* b.   disappear.
c.   increase by 12 points.
d.   vary inversely.

36. The systematic study of the biological basis of all social behavior is called
a.   altruism.
b.   ethology.
c.   ethnography.
* d.   sociobiology.

37. The sociobiological explanation for altruism is that
a.   altruism is the only unselfish act, since an organism sacrifices itself for others.
b.   altruism has never been scientifically established as having occurred in nature.
* c.   organisms sacrifice themselves for close kin who carry many of the same genes.
d.   b and c are true

38. The sociobiological concept of kin selection holds that
* a.   natural selection will preserve altruistic behaviors if the altruists sacrifice themselves for close relatives.
b.   when close relatives interbreed, natural selection causes the harmful recessive alleles to drop out of the population.
c.   when close relatives ally with each other in opposition to outsiders, they will be successful in passing their genetic material on to the next generation.
d.   None of the above is true.

39. Umaru looks up and is horrified to see that, to his left, his sister's child, Fatimatu, is about to be struck by an on-rushing truck, while to his right, his cousin's child, Bouba, has fallen into a flood-swollen stream. He can only try to save one of them, although to save either one will result in his certain death. According to the sociobiological concept of kin selection, which child will he be more likely to save?
   a.　　　Bouba, because he is male
   b.　　　Bouba, because he is closer genetically to Umaru than is Fatimatu
   c.　　　Fatimatu, because she is female
   d　　　Fatimatu, because she is closer genetically to Umaru than is Bouba

40. Why did sociobiology become controversial beginning in the late 1970s?
   a.　　　Sociobiologists had demonstrated that natural selection does not apply to human beings.
* b.　　　Sociobiologists asserted that their approach could be applied to human societies.
   c.　　　Sociobiologists asserted that their research showed that human societies and animal societies were so different as to make comparison impossible.
   d.　　　Sociobiologists were in the forefront of arguing that life on earth was threatened.

41. Which of the following is NOT a requirement for a sociobiological argument explaining the presence of specific physical or behavioral traits?
   a.　　　Variation for the trait existed in the past.
   b.　　　If there was variation in the past, it could be transmitted generationally.
* c.　　　The variation can be explained by individuals' adapting to changes in their environments.
   d.　　　The trait only appears when certain genes are present and is absent when those genes are absent.

42. If evolutionary theory is to explain the openness of human cultural adaptation, it must not only explain _____ patterns of behavior but also _____ ones.
   a.　　　adaptive; reproductive
   b.　　　complex; individual
* c.　　　adaptive; maladaptive
   d.　　　maladaptive; complex

43. According to the text, adopting a rule of thumb is an example of
   a.　　　adaptation.
   b.　　　individual experience.
* c.　　　observational learning.
   d.　　　rational calculation.

38

44. Rachel is a successful lawyer: smart, well-educated, well-connected, extremely hard-working, well-dressed, drives an expensive imported car, and drinks a particular brand of diet cola. When Daniel, who wishes to achieve the same success, imitates as much of Rachel's behavior as he can, including drinking the same diet cola, he is engaged in a form of cultural transmission that Boyd and Richerson call
  a.   flattery.
* b.   indirect bias.
  c.   group selection.
  d.   polygeny.

45. Group selection occurs when
  a.   individuals behave altruistically.
* b.   an individual's fitness depends on the fate of the group to which s/he belongs.
  c.   members of a group work together to insure their survival.
  d.   only certain features of the group are passed on genetically from one generation.

46. When the forces of cultural learning are powerful enough and the fitness of an individual comes to depend on the learned behaviors of other individuals in the group to which s/he belongs, this is known as
  a.   cultural pleiotropy.
* b.   group selection.
  c.   genetic inheritance.
  d.   indirect bias.

47. According to Boyd and Richerson, which of the following inheritance systems shapes human behavior?
  a.   cultural
  b.   genetic
  c.   phenotypic
* d.   both a and b

48. microevolution/macroevolution:
* a.   ecological time/geological time
  b.   groups/individuals
  c.   individual features/group selection
  d.   species/populations

49. anagenesis/cladogenesis:
  a.   species/individual
* b.   single species/multiple species
  c.   gradual change/rapid change
  d.   movement/equilibrium

50. The process by which one species gradually transforms itself into a new species over time is called
  a.   cladogenesis.
  b.   phenotypic transformation.
* c.   phyletic gradualism.
  d.   punctuated equilibrium.

51. Which of the following CANNOT be well explained by phyletic gradualism?
  a.   allelic variation
* b.   cladogenesis
  c.   the way in which one species transforms itself into another over time
  d.   both a and c

52. The process by which a single species gives rise to a variety of descendent species over time is called
  a.   anagenesis.
* b.   cladogensis.
  c.   phyletic gradualism.
  d.   punctuated equilibrium.

53. The theory of punctuated equilibrium is associated with the names of
  a.   Boyd and Richerson.
* b.   Gould and Eldredge.
  c.   Levins and Lewontin.
  d.   Wilson and Lumsden.

54. The theory of punctuated equilibrium is based on the observation that
  a.   brief periods of intense speciation alternate with long periods of stasis.
  b.   new species appear in the fossil record along with their unchanged ancestors.
  c.   evolutionary change does not seem to occur at a constant pace.
* d.   All of the above are true.

55. For punctuationists, the "motor" of speciation is
* a.   drastic environmental change.
   b.   changing gene frequencies.
   c.   an accumulation of mutations and other changes leading to the emergence of a new species.
   d.   all of the above

56. There is increasing evidence that the genetic changes that underlie speciation may be based on
   a.   accumulated small changes in gene frequencies.
* b.   mutuations in regulatory genes that govern the timing of interrelated biological processes.
   c.   radical transformations of the genetic code.
   d.   the need to adapt to dramatically changing environments.

Essay Questions

57. What does it mean to say that populations form a reproductive community?

58. Discuss the role randomness plays in evolution.

59. Discuss the interaction of human cultural practices and biological selection pressures operating on human populations with regard to the sickle-cell genotype.

60. What are the major differences between the phyletic gradualism and punctuated equilibria approaches to interpreting evolution?

61. What are the basic principles of sociobiology? What are the major criticisms of it? What standards must a sociobiological approach to human behavior meet?

62. What is group selection? What makes it a powerful position for understanding the evolution of human culture?

CHAPTER FOUR

THE PRIMATES

Outline

EVOLUTIONARY TRENDS IN PRIMATES

APPROACHES TO PRIMATE TAXONOMY

Phenetics
Cladistics

THE LIVING PRIMATES

Prosimians
Anthropoids

TOPICS IN PRIMATE RESEARCH

Socioecology
Aggression and Affiliation
Intelligence

FLEXIBILITY AS THE HALLMARK OF PRIMATE ADAPTATIONS

Key Terms

morphology	prosimians	dentition
anthropomorphism	anthropoids	sexual dimorphism
stereoscopic vision	hominoids	sexual selection
prehensile	mya	infanticide
diurnal	hominids	socioecology
nocturnal	homology	theory of optimal
taxonomy	analogy	foraging
taxon	cladistics	dominance hierarchy
phenetics	clade	affiliation
grade	ecological niche	grooming behavior

Arguing Anthropology

1. Chimpanzees are so similar to human beings that they have often been used as human stand-ins for experimentation or for testing medications. Is this ethical?

2. What (if anything) can the evidence for aggression and affiliation among nonhuman primates tell us about ourselves.

Multiple Choice Questions

1. Some observers attribute human-like feelings and attitudes to non-human primates because these primates closely resemble human beings in outward physical appearance. This practice is called
   a.   anthropocentrism.
 * b.   anthropomorphism.
   c.   egocentrism.
   d.   ethnocentrism.

2. The study of animal behavior is called
   a.   ethnography.
   b.   ethnology.
 * c.   ethology.
   d.   primatology.

3. Referring to ants, bees, and termites as "social insects" is an example of
   a.   cladistic taxonomy.
   b.   phenetic taxonomy.
   c.   essentialism.
 * d.   metaphor.

4. Which of the following is NOT an ancestral characteristic of primates?
   a.   a collar bone
   b.   five digits on hands and feet
   c.   plantigrade locomotion
 * d.   stereoscopic vision

5. Which of the following is NOT an evolutionary trend in the primate order?
 * a.   reduction in the number of digits on hands and feet
   b.   reduction of the projection of the face
   c.   reduction in the number of teeth
   d.   increase in brain size, relative to body size

6. Which of the following is NOT a unique feature of primates?
 * a.   stereoscopic vision
   b.   presence of nails rather than claws on at least some digits
   c.   opposable thumbs and great toes
   d.   pads at the tips of fingers and toes that are rich in nerve endings

7. LeGros Clark argued that primate evolutionary trends and unique features were the outcome of
* a. an arboreal adaptation.
  b. a diurnal adaptation.
  c. a nocturnal adaptation.
  d. a prehensile adaptation.

8. Matt Cartmill argued that
  a. many other organisms have adapted to life in the trees without having undergone physical and behavioral adaptations similar to the primates.
  b. selective pressure for improved vision resulted from the fact that ancestral primates fed at night and relied on sight to locate their prey.
  c. ancestral primates were adapted to feeding on insects at the ends of tree branches in the lower levels of tropical forests.
* d. All of the above are true.

9. The taxonomy recognized by modern biologists is an inclusive hierarchy because
  a. it groups organisms on the basis of the fewest traits needed to identify the species' essence.
  b. it relies on DNA hybridization to ensure that only those organisms sharing the same essence are included in a species.
* c. lower groups are included within higher groups of the taxonomy.
  d. each organism represents the essence of its own kind, and nothing is related to anything else.

10. Organisms that seem to have developed similar adaptations at a similar level of complexity in similar environments are classified by pheneticists in the same evolutionary
  a. clade.
* b. grade.
  c. taxon.
  d. species.

11. Pheneticists think of evolution primarily as the transformation of a single species over time, or
* a. anagenesis.
  b. cladogenesis.
  c. hybridization.
  d. schismogenesis.

12. Which of the following is NOT a primate grade?
* a.   androids
  b.   hominids
  c.   hominoids
  d.   prosimians

13. A physical similarity between organisms that is the result of genetic inheritance due to common descent is called a(n)
  a.   analogous trait.
* b.   homologous trait.
  c.   phenetic trait.
  d.   hybrid trait.

14. Convergent or parallel evolution results when two species with highly disparate evolutionary histories develop similar physical features as a result of having to adapt to a similar environment. The similar physical features are called
* a.   analogous traits.
  b.   homologous traits.
  c.   phenetic traits.
  d.   hybrid traits.

15. The method of taxonomy known as cladistics classifies living organisms using ONLY
  a.   analogous traits.
* b.   homologous traits.
  c.   phenetic traits.
  d.   hybrid traits.

16. A group of organisms possessing a set of shared, derived features constitute a natural group called a
* a.   clade.
  b.   grade.
  c.   taxon.
  d.   species.

17. Wings in birds and in bats is an example of
* a.   an analogous trait.
  b.   a homologous trait.
  c.   anagenesis.
  d.   cladogenesis.

18. Primates are unlike most mammalian groups because their many-varied species are nearly all found in
     a.   temperate climates.
     b.   tropical climates.
*   c.   aoutheastern Asia.
     d.   Australia.

19. Which prosimian group is native only to the island of Madagascar?
     a.   bushbabies
*   b.   lemurs
     c.   lorises
     d.   tarsiers

20. Which of the following prosimian groups is sometimes grouped together with monkeys and apes, since it appears to share a number of derived traits with them?
     a.   lemurs
     b.   lorises
*   c.   tarsiers
     d.   bushbabies

21. Many prosimian species are nocturnal, which means they
     a.   sleep at night and are active during the day.
*   b.   sleep during the day and are active during the night.
     c.   habitually wash their hands in urine.
     d.   have a moist nose and cleft upper lip.

22. Which of the following factors was probably NOT responsible for helping our primate ancestors to move out of their original niche?
     a.   larger body size
     b.   the ability to eat leaves
     c.   successful competition for diurnal niches with birds
*   d.   large ears that can be moved independently of one another

23. In which of the following prosimians are females individually dominant to males?
     a.   bushbabies
*   b.   lemurs
     c.   lorises
     d.   tarsiers

24. Which of the following is NOT an anthropoid?
   a.   chimpanzee
   b.   howler monkey
   c.   Arnold Schwartzenegger
* d.   None of the above; all are anthropoids

25. platyrrhine:catarrhine::
* a.   New World:Old World
   b.   noctural:diurnal
   c.   Old World:New World
   d.   diurnal:noctural

26. In examining a jaw bone of what is clearly an anthropoid, you observe that
    there are three premolars on each side. You conclude that this is the jawbone
    of a(n)
   a.   catarrhine.
* b.   New World monkey.
   c.   Old World monkey.
   d.   tarsier.

27. New World monkeys differ from Old World monkeys in which of the
    following ways?
* a.   dentition
   b.   diet
   c.   sexual dimorphism
   d.   all of the above

28. When males and females of the same species show observable phenotypic
    differences in, for example, size, the species is said to show
   a.   gender distinctiveness.
   b.   phenotypic magnitude.
   c.   sexual differentiation.
* d.   sexual dimorphism.

29. Howler monkeys are a challenge to analyses that view social organization as
    a by-product of kin selection because the troop is
   a.   only built around the offspring; parents leave the troop after the children
         are sexually mature.
* b.   not built around a core of related females or a core of related males.
   c.   built around brother-brother pairs rather than mother-daughter pairs.
   d.   not built around interacting animals.

30. Colobine monkeys have an important place in contemporary primatology because they have been reported to
   a. emigrate from the troop in which they were born and form random groups.
   b. have completely open hierarchies for both males and females.
 * c. practice infanticide when males from one troop have invaded another troop.
   d. form a clan of related males.

31. Sarah Hardy interprets the disappearance of gray langur infants after invasion of their troop by males from other troops as
   a. adoption.
 * b. infanticide.
   c. paternal investment.
   d. the developmental cycle of langur domestic groups.

32. Sarah Hardy argues that gray langur infanticide makes sense as a reproductive strategy because by killing the unweaned infants in the group that has just been invaded, a male
   a. speeds the conception and birth of his own offspring.
   b. removes the competing offspring of other males.
   c. establishes his dominance.
 * d. both a and b

33. Which of the following has been offered as part of the argument about gray langur infanticide?
   a. Other researchers have not observed infanticide in other gray langur groups.
   b. The infanticide that Hardy analyzes is maladaptive, and the result of overcrowding or human disturbance.
   c. It would be very difficult for males to be able to tell which offspring were theirs.
 * d. All of the above are true.

34. Hamadryas baboons and gelada baboons both live in social groups that possess a single breeding male.
   a. This demonstrates that baboon genetics is at the base of baboon social organization.
   b. The environment is identical for both baboon species.
 * c. Male hamadryas baboons construct their units from unrelated females, whereas female relatives are at the core of gelada baboon social units.
   d. All of the above are true.

35. During the period of female sexual receptivity, male and female baboons typically form temporary pair bonds called
   a.   attachments.
   b.   clans.
* c.   consortships.
   d.   siamangs.

36. Which of the following is a way of distinguishing apes from Old World monkeys?
   a.   absence of tail in apes
   b.   dentition
   c.   skeletal shape
* d.   all of the above

37. Apes are traditionally divided into three families. Which of the following is NOT one of those families?
* a.   Cercopithecoidea
   b.   Hominidae
   c.   Hylobatidae
   d.   Pongidae

38. Biochemical tests and DNA hybridization results show that human beings are most closely related to
   a.   gibbons.
* b.   gorillas.
   c.   orangutans.
   d.   siamangs.

39. A male gibbon
   a.   is smaller than the female.
* b.   has one mate.
   c.   does not defend a territory.
   d.   spends much of his time on the ground.

40. Among gorillas
   a.   only males transfer out of the group in which they were born.
   b.   only females transfer out of the group in which they were born.
* c.   both females and males transfer out of the group in which they were born.
   d.   transfer out of the group in which they were born is random for both sexes.

41. Adult male gorillas
   a.   are much larger than females.
   b.   treat immature gorillas with tolerance.
   c.   eat primarily meat.
* d.   both a and b

42. BOTH chimpanzees and bonobos
   a.   use sex as a way of manipulating social relationships.
   b.   are native to Africa.
   c.   use sticks to "fish" for insects in termite mounds and anthills.
* d.   both a and b

43. Which of the following primate groups apparently uses sexual behavior to manipulate relationships rather than to increase reproductive rates?
   a.   gibbons
   b.   gorillas
* c.   bonobos
   d.   chimpanzees

44. Primatologists who try to explain different forms of primate society by relating them to the different environment in which each primate species typically lives and to the food it typically eats, are called
   a.   sociobiologists.
* b.   socioecologists.
   c.   environmentalists.
   d.   paleobotanists.

45. A primate whose diet emphasizes animal food is called
   a.   folivorous
* b.   faunivorous
   c.   frugivorous
   d.   herbivorous

46. A major difficulty besetting primatologists trying to classify different primate diets is the fact that
   a.   it is impossible to collect data on primate diets.
* b.   the primate order as a whole is characterized by omnivory.
   c.   it is extremely difficult to distinguish frugivorous and folivorous diets.
   d.   few primates are vegetarians.

47. The theory of optimal foraging claims that primates will maximize the amount

a. of protein in their diet.

b. of fruit they consume before they turn to other kinds of food.

* c. and quality of food they eat while minimizing the effort to find such food.

d. of time they can devote to free play by minimizing the time they devote to the food quest.

48. Feeding "efficiency" of primates is difficult to measure in the wild because

a. it is extremely difficult to determine what constitutes an adequate diet for members of a particular primate species.

b. it is difficult to discover the nutritional content of different primate diets because it is hard to measure the rate at which fixed amounts of particular foods are consumed in the wild.

c. measures of adequate diet must distinguish between undernourishment and malnourishment, which is difficult.

* d. All of the above are true.

49. Socioecology

a. tends toward environmental determinism.

b. accounts for species diversity by attributing it to divergent adaptations by different species to different ecological niches.

c. cannot explain why variations in foraging behavior continue to be found in species that are supposedly optimally adapted to a given niche.

* d. all of the above

50. Brown lemurs of Madagascar eat primarily mature leaves yet grind up and digest this food less efficiently than ring-tailed lemurs, who eat primarily fruit, flowers, and young leaves, which are more easily digested. Alison Richard explains this state of affairs by claiming

a. that brown lemurs have evolved specialized teeth and a specialized gut designed to handle the high cellulose content of a leaf diet.

b. brown lemurs are bound to become extinct as they are outcompeted by ring-tailed lemurs.

c. both species are most likely getting by and making ecological experiments after two thousand years of rapid change.

d. suboptimal members of a population who perform better than optimal members in marginal environments are of no importance in evolution.

51. Socioecological studies have made primatologists aware that
* a.   "normal" behavior or the "natural" environment for a particular primate species is not at all self-evident.
  b.   primates with the morphology of "vertical clingers and leapers" are in fact narrowly restricted in their ability to reach certain food sources.
  c.   sociobiological explanations and socioecological explanations do not compete with one another, but in fact explain entirely different aspects of primate behavior.
  d.   the existing conditions in which a primate species lives always represent adaptive success.

52. Primatologists who study primate aggression
  a.   all agree about what constitutes an example of aggressive behavior.
  b.   have clearly shown that a male's dominance rank correlates with his reproductive success.
  c.   are only interested in the ability of one individual to dominate another individual.
* d.   have shown that females of different species vary in their dependence on males for protection.

53. Which of the following behaviors has been used to measure dominance in primates?
  a.   acting to defend the group
  b.   breaking up fights between other group members
  c.   leading the group
* d.   all of the above

54. Measuring dominance in primate groups is difficult because
  a.   different behaviors are used to measure dominance.
  b.   different individuals (of different sexes) may show different dominance behaviors in different contexts.
  c.   sometimes individuals band together for defense or attack.
* d.   All of the above are true.

55. Grooming behavior is of interest to primatologists because it is
* a.   an important way of creating friendly relationships between animals that might otherwise be hostile to one another.
  b.   restricted to mothers and their offspring.
  c.   only used between males who are normally aggressive to one another.
  d.   not found in primate groups that have dominance hierarchies.

56. The transfer of information from one individual to another is a definition of
* a.   communication.
  b.   language.
  c.   speech.
  d.   intelligence.

57. Attempts to teach apes to use sign language show that
  a.   apes are ill-suited to use sign language because they have so little
         control over their gestures.
* b.   primatologists do not agree that apes combine signs according to
         grammatical rules.
  c.   apes communicate better with human beings using sign language than
         they do using computer keyboards.
  d.   ape linguistic abilities are better demonstrated when they use computer
         keyboards than when they are taught sign language.

58. Laboratory tests suggest that those primates that show the most curiosity
    and perform best on tests that require exploration and manipulation of
    apparatus are species
  a.   whose natural habitats are bland and uniform.
* b.   that rely on varied and opportunistic feeding strategies in the wild.
  c.   that are born and raised in captivity.
  d.   that have been trained to use American Sign Language.

59. Much of the intelligence primates show in the wild seems to deal with
* a.   their knowledge and manipulation of social relationships.
  b.   their need to cope with the complexities of rain forest ecology.
  c.   their need to avoid predators.
  d.   the challenge of hunting for animal prey.

60. According to Frans de Waal, the biological basis of primate social skills
    like conflict resolution and reconciliation requires the ability to
  a.   recognize individual animals and a good memory.
  b.   shift fairly quickly from hostile to friendly feelings.
  c.   be soothed by bodily contact or certain visual signals.
* d.   all of the above

61. Overall, the studies of primatologists suggest that primate adaptations are
  a.   marked by flexibility.
  b.   tightly controlled by genes.
  c.   narrowly restricted by environmental conditions.
  d.   heavily conditioned by limited opportunities for reproductive success.

Essay Questions

62. What are the drawbacks of anthropomorphizing nonhuman primates?

63. Choose two or three of the evolutionary trends that have appeared in primates, define them, and describe them. Why are they important?

64. What are the differences between clades and grades? Why are the differences important?

65. Choose two or three nonhuman primate species and discuss the relations between males and females in each species. What kinds of reasons can be suggested for (a) the differences between and among the species and (b) between males and females in each species?

66. Discuss gray langur infanticide. What reasons have been proposed to explain it?

67. Compare and contrast socioecological and sociobiological theories of primate behavior? What are the advantages and disadvantages of each approach?

68. Discuss some of the research directed toward the study of aggression and affiliation in nonhuman primates. What are some of the arguments made about aggression? What are some of the alternative explanations that have been offered? Which positions do you find more compelling? Why?

69. What are the areas in which nonhuman primate intelligence has been tested? What have been the results of the research into nonhuman primate intelligence?

CHAPTER 5

STUDYING THE HUMAN PAST

Outline

INTERPRETING THE PREHISTORIC RECORD

DATING METHODS

Relative Dating Methods
Chronometric Dating Methods
Reconstructing Prehistoric Climates

ARCHAEOLOGY

Survey Archaeology
Archaeological Excavation

CONTEMPORARY TRENDS

Feminist Archaeology
Collaborative Approaches to Studying the Past

Key Terms

artifacts
archaeological record
relative dating
chronometric dating
stratum
law of superposition
law of crosscutting
  relationships
biostratigraphic dating

seriation
radiometric dating
  methods
nonradiometric methods
  of chronometric dating
site
region
features

ethnoarchaeology
taphonomy
survey
excavation
assemblage
archaeological culture
feminist archaeology
historical archaeology

Arguing Anthropology

1. In recent years, state and federal laws have mandated that the remains of indigenous people of North America found in archaeological or scientific collections be returned to contemporary Indian peoples or appropriate agencies so that those remains can be reburied. Are there any circumstances in which archaeological excavation of human burials is justified?

2. Since archaeological excavation destroys the past as it reveals it, should archaeologists stop excavating until better non-destructive technologies are developed?

Multiple Choice

1. Material evidence of human modification of the material environment over time is called
   a.   the fossil record.
   * b.   the archaeological record.
   c.   the paleontological record.
   d.   the phenetic record.

2. Dating methods that identify a particular object as being older or younger in relation to some other object, and that arrange material evidence in a linear sequence, so that we know what came before what, are called
   a.   chronometric dating methods.
   b.   chronotopic dating methods.
   * c.   relative dating methods.
   d.   allometric dating methods.

3. Dating methods based on laboratory treatment or analysis of various items recovered from an excavation that can tell us, for example, how many years ago a rock layer formed, are called
   * a.   chronometric dating methods.
   b.   chronotopic dating methods.
   c.   relative dating methods.
   d.   allometric dating methods.

4. A layer-cake profile of different soil types is exposed when we dig into the earth. Geologists reasoned that these layers were laid down sequentially, and that layers lower down had to be older than the layers above them. This is called
   * a.   the Law of Superposition.
   b.   the Law of Cross-Cutting Relationships.
   c.   the Law of the Jungle.
   d.   the Law of Unconformities.

5. Sometimes old rocks are affected by other geological features, as when molten lava forces its way through fractures in several superposed layers on its way to the surface. The assumption that the intruding features must be younger than the layers of rock on which they intrude is called
   a.   the Law of Superposition.
   * b.   the Law of Cross-Cutting Relationships.
   c.   the Law of the Land.
   d.   the Law of Unconformities.

6. In the eighteenth century, Georges Cuvier and his associate Alexandre Brongniart made independent collections of rock and fossil samples from the same deposits in the Seine River Basin near Paris. When they compared the two collections, they discovered that
   a. there was no correlation among fossils, rock samples, and strata.
 * b. certain fossils were always found in certain strata but not it others.
   c. fossils in lower strata looked more like living animals than did those in higher strata.
   d. both a and c

7. In the early 1900s, fluorine analysis helped paleoanthropologists prove that a famous fossil hominid called "Piltdown man" was a forgery because
   a. the flourine level in the skull was the same as the flourine level of other bones from the Piltdown site.
   b. the skull and the jaw had similar fluorine levels, but these were different from the fluorine levels found in other bones from the Piltdown site.
   c. the skull and jaw had no accumulated fluorine, whereas other bones from the Piltdown site had high levels of fluorine.
 * d. the fluorine level present in the skull was different from that found in the jaw, and neither level corresponded to the amount of fluorine found in other bones from the Piltdown site.

8. Relative dating that relies on patterns of fossil distribution in different rock layers is called
   a. serial dating.
   b. blind dating.
 * c. biostratigraphic dating.
   d. typological dating.

9. What role was played by fossils of the one-toed horse when paleoanthropologists tried to assign firm dates to hominid-fossil-bearing layers at the Eastern African site of Koobi Fora?
   a. If the potassium-argon date at Koobi Fora was correct, then these fossils appeared at Koobi Fora more than half a million years earlier than they appeared in the Lower Omo Valley, 100 kilometers to the north.
   b. The presence of these fossils at Koobi Fora, but not at Omo, convinced paleoanthropologists that previous biostratigraphy at the two sites was mistaken.
   c. Cross-checking chronometric dates and biostratigraphy involving these fossils caused paleoanthropologists to question the potassium-argon date for Koobi Fora.
   d. Both a and c are true.

10. Sometimes archaeologists create typological sequences of artifacts, assuming that artifacts that look alike were made at the same time, and that artifact styles evolve slowly. This is called
   a.   biostratigraphy.
* b.   seriation.
   c.   cladistics.
   d.   superposition.

11. Some chronometric dating methods are based on scientific knowledge about the rate at which various radioactive isotopes of naturally occurring elements transform themselves into other elements by losing subatomic particles. These are known as
   a.   relative dating methods.
   b.   cladistic dating methods.
* c.   radiometric dating methods.
   d.   serial dating methods.

12. Rates of radioactive decay make useful atomic clocks because
   a.   as far as we know, they are unaffected by other physical or chemical processes.
   b.   we can use dates obtained by one radiometric method to cross-check dates obtained by other radiometric methods.
   c.   the fact that different radiometric methods regularly agree indicates that radioactive dating is self-consistent and reassures us that we are measuring real ages.
* d.   All of the above are true.

13. Which dating method is accurate for dates from the origin of the earth up to about 100,000 years ago and is used to date layers of volcanic rock?
* a.   potassium-argon dating
   b.   fission-track dating
   c.   uranium-series dating
   d.   radiocarbon dating

14. Which dating method can be used to date soil deposits, such as limestones, that formed in ancient sea or lake beds?
   a.   potassium-argon dating
   b.   fission-track dating
* c.   uranium-series dating
   d.   radiocarbon dating

15. Which dating method is useful for dating the remains of organisms that died as long ago as 30,000 to 40,000 years ago? (A refined version of this method can date organic materials that are 50,000 to 80,000 years old.)
   a.   potassium-argon dating
   b.   fission-track dating
   c.   uranium-series dating
* d.   radiocarbon dating

16. Which dating method provides dates between 40,000 and 100,000-300,000 years ago, and enables us to determine the date when ancient pottery fragments were last fired, or when burnt-flint artifacts last were heated?
* a.   thermoluminescence
   b.   electron-spin resonance
   c.   dendrochronology
   d.   radiocarbon dating

17. Which dating method can provide dates ranging from a few thousand to a million years ago, measures the number of electrons trapped within a sample, and may prove most helpful in dating specimens of bone and teeth?
   a   thermoluminescence
* b.   electron-spin resonance
   c.   dendrochronology
   d.   radiocarbon dating

18. Which of the following is a nonradiometric method of chronometric dating?
   a.   thermoluminescence
   b.   electron-spin resonance
* c.   dendrochronology
   d.   radiocarbon dating

19. The dating method that uses tree ring patterns to construct a master sequence that can be used to date wood recovered from archaeological sites is called
   a.   thermoluminescence.
   b.   electron-spin resonance.
* c.   dendrochronology.
   d.   radiocarbon dating.

20. Paleomagnetism is a dating method based on changes in the earth's polarity as demonstrated by

a.   regular changes in soil types in a stratigraphic sequence.

b.   sequences of thin and thick layers of sediment in ancient lake or sea beds.

c.   changing concentrations of salt in layers of polar ice.

* d.   changing directions of alignment of particles in volcanic rocks or fine-grained sediments.

21. Paleomagnetism is valuable because it is the only dating method that

a.   provides absolute dates for fossil deposits laid down during the crucial period between 500,000 and 50,000 years ago.

* b.   has the potential to provide a temporal framework within which geological, climatological, and evolutionary events can be related on a worldwide scale.

c.   provides absolute dates for clay artifacts.

d.   can date organic remains that fossilized more than 100,000 years ago.

22. The molecular clock is based on the assumption that

a.   living organisms have equal amounts of carbon and carbon-14 in their tissues.

* b.   genetic mutations accumulate at a constant rate.

c.   the products of uranium decay tend to solidify, separate out of water, and mix with salts that collect on the bottom of a lake or sea.

d.   heating an irradiated substance releases trapped electrons together with a quantity of light directly in proportion to their number.

23. Which of the following is a criticism of the molecular clock as a dating technique?

a.   The proportion of carbon 14 in the atmosphere may change from one period of prehistory to another.

b   Contamination by sources of uranium other than water may affect the accuracy of the dating method.

* c.   The accuracy of the molecular clock depends on the accuracy of some other chronometric method used to date the presumed fossil ancestors of one of the species being compared.

d.   The molecular clock is unreliable because it dates rocks, not organic remains.

24. Information about ancient climates is important to paleoanthropologists because
    a.   climate fluctuations may correlate with important evolutionary events, such as extinction or diversification of species.
    b.   this information helps us to reconstruct the selective pressures that eventually gave rise to our own species.
    c.   it allows us to distinguish chrons from subchrons.
*   d.   both a and b

25. Anthropologists who specialize in the interpretation of cultural variation and cultural change in the human past are called
    a.   paleoanthropologists.
    b.   paleontologists.
    c.   cultural anthropologists.
*   d.   archaeologists.

26. The study of the way people in present-day societies use artifacts and structures on the sites where they live, and how these objects become part of the archaeological record is called
*   a.   ethnoarchaeology.
    b.   taphonomy.
    c.   survey archaeology.
    d.   excavation.

27. The study of the various processes that affect the formation of a particular site, explaining how certain objects in that site (such as bones or stone tools) came to be where they are found, is called
    a.   ethnoarchaeology.
*   b.   taphonomy.
    c.   survey archaeology.
    d.   excavation.

28. Which of the following factors prevents artifacts from decaying?
    a.   extreme cold
    b.   extreme heat and dryness
    c.   waterlogged sites free of oxygen
*   d.   all of the above

29. The study of site types, their distribution, and their layouts is called
    a.   ethnoarchaeology.
    b.   taphonomy.
*   c.   survey archaeology.
    d.   excavation.

30. The systematic uncovering of archaeological remains through the removal of the deposits of soil and other material covering them and accompanying them is called
   a.   ethnoarchaeology.
   b.   taphonomy.
   c.   survey archaeology.
* d.   excavation.

31. When artifacts and structures from a particular time and place are grouped together, they are called
* a.   an assemblage.
   b.   an archaeological culture.
   c.   an artifact distribution.
   d.   a material culture.

32. Ian Hodder's work among several contemporary ethnic groups in Eastern Africa showed that
   a.   tool styles were symbols of group identity.
   b.   pottery styles were symbols of group identity.
* c.   ear ornaments were symbols of group identity.
   d.   contemporary distribution of pottery styles corresponded to patterns of pottery style distribution discovered in the archaeological record of this region.

33. Ian Hodder warns archaeologists they may make serious errors if
   a.   they fail to recognize that the distribution of tool styles is the most reliable indicator of the boundaries of archaeological cultures.
   b.   they fail to realize that archaeological cultures are the product of scientific analysis and are not obvious from the archaeological record alone.
   c.   they fail to realize that only items of material culture that serve as symbols of group identity are reliable indicators of cultural boundaries.
* d.   both b and c

34. Feminist archaeology
   a   actively explores the reasons why women's contributions have been systematically written out of the archaeological record.
   b.   replaces focus on remains with focus on people as active social agents.
   c.   rejects traditional archaeological assumptions that human adaptation can be exhaustively explained in terms of climate, ecology, and technology.
* d.   All of the above are true.

35. Rita Wright argues that archaeologists should NOT assume that women's contributions to pottery production ceased once it became a highly developed commercial activity in early state societies because
   a.   her work in the Andes shows that pottery factories in Inca times were entirely in the hands of women.
 * b.   pottery production often depends on a cooperative labor force and therefore a division of labor into various tasks, some or all of which women have performed in historically known pottery-producing societies.
   c.   women invented the potter's wheel.
   d.   her work in Egypt shows that clay preparation remained the work of women for more than 1000 years.

36. According to the text, the greatest challenge to male bias in archaeological interpretation concerns the roles women played in
   a.   pottery production.
 * b.   stone-tool manufacture.
   c.   hunting.
   d.   textile production.

37. Traditional archaeological interpretations of stone tools
   a.   favor highly formalized, elaborately retouched, standardized core tools.
   b.   assume that stone tools were made for men to hunt with.
   c.   downplay or ignore the numerous flake tools that are found in sites.
 * d.   All of the above are true.

38. Joan Gero's analysis of stone-tool use over time at the site of Huaricoto in highland Peru argues that
   a.   female status may have been connected to stone-tool production during the early period, when the site was a ceremonial center.
   b.   female status may have been shifted to ceramic production during the later period, when the site had become a village settlement.
   c.   male status in the early period may have been connected to ceramic production during the early period, when the site was a ceremonial center.
 * d.   women probably made and used stone tools during the later period, when the site had become a village settlement, but they were utilitarian flake tools.

39. Janet Spector's excavation of a site near Jordan, Minnesota focused on

a.   prehistory.

* b.   post-European contact between indigenous people and settlers.

c.   changes in stone-tool use at the site from prehistoric times until the nineteenth century.

d.   changes in textile production at the site from prehistoric times until the nineteenth century.

40. Janet Spector's archaeological work was unusual because

a.   she was the first woman ever to direct an archaeological excavation.

* b.   Dakota and non-Dakota were collaborating in teaching Dakota language, oral history, ethnobotany, ecology, and history at the site while digging continued.

c.   her work brought to light detailed information about technological changes in Dakota textile production that had never before been documented archaeologically.

d.   she was able to show that stone-tool manufacture and use remained important at Village at the Rapids, even after settlers began importing metal tools.

Essay Questions

41. What are the different advantages and drawbacks of relative and chronometric dating methods?

42. Compare and contrast archaeological survey work and excavation. What are the strengths and weaknesses of each?

43. What are the principal points made by feminist archaeologists regarding the goals of archaeology?

44. How do collaborative approaches to studying the past change the way archaeology is practiced?

CHAPTER 6

PRIMATE EVOLUTION

Outline

PRIMATE EVOLUTION: THE FIRST FIFTY-FIVE MILLION YEARS

PRIMATES OF PALEOCENE: NEW QUESTIONS

PRIMATES OF THE EOCENE: THE FIRST PROSIMIANS

PRIMATES OF THE OLIGOCENE: THE FIRST ANTHROPOIDS

PRIMATES OF THE MIOCENE: THE ANCESTORS OF MODERN
    MONKEYS AND APES

RELATIONS BETWEEN LATE MIOCENE HOMINOIDS AND EARLY
    HOMINIDS

Key Terms

primates of modern
    aspect
cranium
postcranial skeleton
holotype

catarrhines
platyrrhines
Aegyptopithecus
Y-5 molar

bilophodont molar
hominoids
Proconsul
evolutionary mosaic

Arguing Anthropology

1. What good is fossil evidence?

2. The concept of an "evolutionary mosaic" is a provocative and powerful one.
   Why?

Multiple Choice

1. Morphological similarities between fossils that are the result of parallel or
   convergent evolution, as unrelated species adapted to similar environments,
   are called

* a.   analogous traits.
   b.   homologous traits.
   c.   homozygous traits.
   d.   heterozygous traits.

2. Morphological similarities between fossils that are the result of common ancestry are called
   a. analogous traits.
 * b. homologous traits.
   c. homozygous traits.
   d. heterozygous traits.

3. Species that are morphologically indistinguishable and can only be identified in the wild on the basis of mating behavior and geographical distribution are called
   a. analogous species.
   b. homologous species.
 * c. sibling species.
   d. cousin species.

4. The comparison made by Eldredge and Tattersall between living lions and tigers and the bones of lions and tigers shows that
   a. lions and tigers are analogous species.
   b. lions and tigers are homologous species.
   c. lions and tigers are sibling species.
 * d. species boundaries are not always marked by morphological differences in skeletal structure.

5. Fossil primates that look enough like living primates to be classified as their probable ancestors are called
   a. analogous species.
   b. homologous species.
   c. sibling species.
 * d. primates of modern aspect.

6. R. D. Martin points out that failure to acknowledge major gaps in the fossil record can lead to
   a. incorrect lumping together of analogous species.
   b. incorrect splitting apart of sibling species.
 * c. serious underestimation of how long ago species shared a common ancestor.
   d. overestimation of the number of hominid species that have lived since the hominid line first appeared some 5 to 8 million years ago.

7. The bones of an animal's head are called its
 * a. cranium.
   b. postcranial skeleton.
   c. holotype.
   c. taxon.

8. The bones of an animal's body, not including its head, are called its
   a.   cranium.
 * b.   postcranial skeleton.
   c.   holotype.
   d.   taxon.

9. The best or most complete examples of a particular fossil, which is used as a standard against which future, similar finds will be compared, is called a
   a.   cranium.
   b.   postcranial skeleton.
 * c.   holotype.
   d.   taxon.

10. Recent fossil discoveries and analyses now suggest that the plesiadapiforms are NOT related to the primates because
   a.   their cranial skeleton is very different from primate crania.
   b.   their postcranial skeleton is very different from the postcranial skeletons of primates.
 * c.   the auditory bulla is formed differently in plesiadapiforms from the way it is formed in primates.
   d.   the cheek teeth of plesiadapiforms are very different from the cheek teeth of primates.

11. The Eocene epoch, which lasted from about 54 mya to about 38 mya, witnessed the appearance and spread of
   a.   the first plesiadapiforms.
 * b.   the first primates of modern aspect.
   c.   the first anthropoids.
   d.   the first catarrhines.

12. Which of the following morphological traits is NOT shared by modern lemurs and Eocene lemurs?
   a.   large, forward-facing eyes
   b.   primate structure of the auditory bulla
   c.   distinctive wrist and ankle morphology
 * d.   a long snout, with eye orbits placed on the sides of the skull

13. The first primates of modern aspect to appear in the fossil record are fossil
   a.   anthropoids.
   b.   catarrhines.
   c.   platyrrhines.
 * d.   prosimians.

14. The anatomical attributes of the earliest primates is currently explained as the result of a new adaptation to
   a.   life in the trees.
* b.   feeding at night on insects at the ends of branches in the lower levels of the tropical forest.
   c.   diurnal feeding on insects living under the bark of tropical trees.
   d.   life on the ground.

15. Which of the following features is found in modern prosimians but NOT in their fossil ancestors?
   a.   four premolars
* b.   a tooth comb
   c.   generalized incisors and canines
   d.   forward-facing eyes

16. Prosimians became fewer and less diverse, and the first anthropoids flourished during which epoch?
   a.   Eocene
* b.   Oligocene
   c.   Miocene
   d.   Paleocene

17. Old World anthropoids (including monkeys, apes, and human beings) are also known as
* a.   catarrhines.
   b.   platyrrhines.
   c.   cercopithecoids.
   d.   androids.

18. New World anthropoids, all of which are considered monkeys, are also known as
   a.   catarrhines.
* b.   platyrrhines.
   c.   cercopithecoids.
   d.   androids.

19. The Fayum Depression in Egypt
a.   produced the most complete fossils of plesiadapiforms dating from the Paleocene.
b.   is a key site for fossils showing the appearance of the first anthropoids during the Miocene.
c.   is a rich source of prosimian fossils dating from the Oligocene.
* d.   is a rich source of fossil evidence of anthropoid evolution in the Oligocene.

20. The best-known of the Oligocene fossil anthropoids is called
a.   *Plesiadapis*
b.   *Prosimius*
* c.   *Aegyptopithecus*
d.   *Proconsul*

21. Bilophodont molars are now believed to be
a.   uniquely derived traits of apes and human beings.
b.   primitive for all Old World anthropoids.
* c.   derived traits of Old World monkeys.
d.   uniquely derived traits of New World monkeys.

22. Since *Aegyptopithecus* had two premolars, rather than three, it CANNOT be ancestral to
a.   apes.
b.   Old World anthropoids.
* c.   New World anthropoids.
d.   human beings.

23. Y-5 molars are NOT found in which of the following primate groups?
a.   prosimians
b.   Old World Monkeys
c.   New World Monkeys
* d.   all of the above

24. Which tooth type is shared by *Aegyptopithecus* and human beings?
a.   none
* b.   y-5 molar
c.   bilophodont molar
d.   third premolar

25. *Aegyptopithecus* is now thought to be ancestral to
   a.   later Old World monkeys.
   b.   later New World monkeys.
   c.   later apes.
* d.   both a and c

26. The appearance of bilophodont molars may be associated with
* a.   a shift from a fruit-based to a leaf-based diet in early cercopithecoid monkeys.
   b.   a shift from a leaf-based diet in early apes to a diet of fruits with hard coverings or seeds.
   c.   a shift from an insect-based diet to a fruit-based diet in the first New World monkeys.
   d.   a shift from a fruit-based diet to an insect-based diet in the first anthropoids.

27. According to Alfred Rosenberger, which of the following features does NOT describe anthropoid dental morphology?
   a.   incisors used for biting
   b.   premolars used for crushing
   c.   molars used for crushing and grinding
* d.   dentition used for shearing and puncturing

28. The anthropoid jaw and skull are both fused along the midlines, and the orbits are enclosed by bony plates. This is interpreted by Rosenberger as evidence for
   a.   adaptation to a diet based on fruit or leaves.
* b.   adaptation to a diet based on fruits with hard coverings or seeds.
   c.   adaptation to a diet based primarily on meat.
   d.   adaptation to a diet based primarily on insects.

29. The fact that the anthropoid jaw and skull are both fused along the midlines makes them
   a.   less able to withstand physical stresses of biting, crushing, and grinding food.
* b.   stronger and better able to withstand physical stresses of biting, crushing, and grinding food.
   c.   weaker than the prosimian jaw and skull.
   d.   both a and c

30. Which of the following statements does NOT describe the morphology of *Aegyptopithecus?*
   a.   It looks very much like a primitive monkey.
* b.   Its limb bones show features that would have allowed it to hang upright or swing from the branches of trees.
   c.   Compared to modern anthropoids, its brain was smaller.
   d.   Its teeth were extremely apelike.

31. Recent fossil discoveries in the Fayum and in Algeria suggest that
   a.   anthropoids appeared later on the scene than Elwyn Simons first suggested.
* b.   anthropoids and prosimians may have appeared on the scene at roughly the same time, during the Paleocene.
   c.   prosimians were more plentiful in the Oligocene than was previously realized.
   d.   monkeys and prosimians may have appeared on the scene at roughly the same time, during the Eocene.

32. Currently, primatologists believe that Old World and New World monkeys
   a.   originated on separate continents, each evolving from earlier local prosimian populations.
* b.   both shared a common ancestor that first appeared in the Old World.
   c.   are more closely related to one another than Old World monkeys are related to apes.
   d.   both shared a common ancestor that first appeared in South America.

33. The Miocene epoch shows the first fossil evidence of
   a.   lemurs.
   b.   catarrhines.
   c.   platyrrhines.
* d.   hominoids.

34. The first hominoids appeared in
* a.   Africa.
   b.   Asia.
   c.   South America.
   d.   Europe.

35. A land bridge that formed around 18 to 17 mya joined the African plate (including the Arabian peninsula) to the Eurasian plate. This is responsible for
* a.   making the climate cooler and drier.
   b.   making the climate warmer and wetter.
   c.   allowing hominoids to enter Africa for the first time.
   d.   both b and c

36. Primate paleontologists have come to use the appearance of the African-Eurasian land bridge to divide the early Miocene from the middle Miocene. They also distinguish a late Miocene period, characterized by
   a.   unprecedented success of Old World monkeys.
   b.   the extinction of many hominoid species.
   c.   the first appearance of the hominids.
* d.   all of the above

37. One of the best-known early Miocene hominoids is
   a.   *Plesiadapis*
   b.   *Aegyptopithecus*
   c.   *Promisius*
* d.   *Proconsul*

38. A phenotypic pattern that shows how different traits of an organism, responding to different selection pressures, may evolve at different rates, is called
* a.   an evolutionary mosaic.
   b.   a missing link.
   c.   a sibling species.
   d.   an analogous trait.

39. Which of the following features describes *Proconsul africanus?*
   a.   It is very apelike in the morphology of its cranium.
   b.   It is very apelike in its shoulder and elbow joints.
   c.   Its trunk and the bones of its arm and hand resemble those of modern monkeys.
* d.   all of the above

40. The fossils of *Proconsul* have been found in
* a.   Africa.
   b.   Asia.
   c.   Europe.
   d.   all of the above

41. During the middle Miocene
   a.   the climate throughout the Old World became warmer and wetter.
 * b.   hominoids spread throughout the Old World, radiating into many habitats.
   c.   the number of hominoid species decreased.
   d.   hominoid fossils from Africa outnumber hominoid fossils from elsewhere in the Old World.

42. Which of the following fossil hominoids was once thought to be the first member of the hominid line?
   a.   *Aegyptopithecus*
   b.   *Proconsul*
 * c.   *Ramapithecus*
   d.   *Dryopithecus*

43. Some primate paleontologists argued that perhaps *Sivapithecus* was ancestral both to orangutans and to human beings, because
   a.   *Sivapithecus* was ancestral both to *Ramapithecus* and to the hominids.
   b.   molecular evidence suggested that modern human beings were more closely related to orangutans than to African apes.
   c.   hominid fossils found in the 1970s showed many postcranial similarities to orangutans.
 * d.   both modern orangutans and the earliest hominids had thick enamel on their molars.

44. Which statement reflects current thinking about enamel thickness on molars and hominid evolution?
   a.   Thick molar enamel can form in only one way.
 * b.   The ancestors of African apes probably had thick enamel.
   c.   The thick enamel of modern African apes is a more recent, derived trait.
   d.   The earliest hominids had thin enamel.

45. Which of the following best describes current attempts to classify Miocene hominoids?
   a.   All of these fossils have been assigned either to the genus *Dryopithecus* or to the genus *Ramapithecus*.
   b.   Fossils assigned to *Ramapithecus* flourished in Europe, whereas fossils assigned to *Dryopithecus* flourished in Asia.
 * c.   Miocene hominoids vary so enormously that many paleontologists are unwilling to classify them beyond the level of the genus, and none of the genera they recognize are claimed as direct ancestors of the hominids.
   d.   both a and b

46. Currently, what do most paleoanthropologists believe about the relations between late Miocene hominoids and early hominids?
* a. Chimpanzees, gorillas, and human beings shared a common ancestor in the late Miocene.
  b. Orangutans and human beings shared a common ancestor in the late Miocene.
  c. The best candidate for our first hominid ancestor is *Ramapithecus*.
  d. None of the above is true.

Essay Questions

47. What is the significance of *Aegyptopithecus* in the evolutionary history of the primates? Be sure to present specific details.

48. What sort of evolutionary pressures may have produced the earliest anthropoids?

49. Why have paleontologists rejected the parallel evolution interpretation for the relationship between Old World and New World monkeys?

50. Discuss the importance of the Miocene period in the evolution of primates. Pay particular attention to the relevant fossils as well as natural selection pressures during the period.

CHAPTER 7

HOMINID EVOLUTION

Outline

THE EARLY AUSTRALOPITHECINES (4–3 mya)

HOMINID EVOLUTION

The Origin of Bipedalism
Changes in Hominid Dentition

THE LATER AUSTRALOPITHECINES (3–2.5 mya)

How Many Species of Later Australopithecines Were There?
Australopithecines: Clade or Grade?
Expansion of the Australopithecine Brain

EARLY *HOMO* SPECIES (2–1.6 mya)

Earliest Evidence of Culture: Stone tools of the Oldowan Tradition

EXPLAINING THE HUMAN TRANSITION

Models from Primatology

Models from Ethnography

HOMO ERECTUS (1.8–1.7 MYA TO .5–.4 MYA)

Morphological Traits of *Homo Erectus*
The Culture of *Homo Erectus*
Homo Erectus the Forager?

THE EVOLUTIONARY FATE OF *HOMO ERECTUS*

Key Terms

bipedalism
hominids
australopithecines
foramen magnum
valgus angle
diasterna
gracile australopithecines
robust australopithecines
cranial capacity
masseter muscle

zygomatic arch
temporal muscle
sagittal crest
breccia
morphological space
Homo habilis
postorbital constriction
cores
flakes
Oldowan tradition

taphonomy
foraging societies
Homo erectus
basicranial flexion
Acheulean tradition
Lower Paleolithic
Early Stone Age
Asian chopper/chopping
    tool assemblages

Arguing Anthropology

1. Why should anyone care whether our ancestors hunted or scavenged?

2. Given the evidence in the text, which scenarios of early hominid life seem most reasonable to you? Why?

Multiple Choice Questions

1. Walking on two feet rather than four is called
* a.   bipedalism.
  b.   quadrupedalism.
  c.   bipolarism.
  d.   taphonomy.

2. Primates that walk on two feet are called
  a.   anthropoids.
  b.   apes.
  c.   hominoids.
* d.   hominids.

3. Which of the following is NOT considered one of the four important areas of hominid evolution?
  a.   bipedal locomotion
  b.   expanded brain
  c.   changes in dentition
* d.   loss of body fur

4. The oldest known hominids, dating between 4 and 3 million years of age, are called
  a.   anthropoids.
* b.   australopithecines.
  c.   hominines.
  d.   australoids.

5. Which of the following is NOT considered an advantage of bipedalism over quadrupedalism?
* a.   the ability to climb trees
  b.   the ability to spot predators easily in open country
  c.   the ability to escape more easily from predators in open country
  d.   the ability to cover greater distances with greater energy efficiency, although at lower speeds

6. The teeth of the first bipedal hominids were probably adapted to
   a. an exclusively carnivorous diet.
   b. an exclusively vegetarian diet.
 * c. an omnivorous diet.
   d. endurance hunting.

7. According to Isaac and Crader, it appears that the first hominids
   a. preferred forest environments.
   b. preferred grassland environments.
   c. preferred swamps.
 * d. ranged widely over varied environments.

8. The earliest evidence we have of hominid bipedalism comes from
   a. fossilized knee bones.
 * b. fossilized footprints.
   c. fossilized foot bones.
   d. fossilized pelvic bones.

9. The earliest hominid skeletal fossils showing evidence of a bipedal
   adaptation have been assigned to the species
 * a. *Australopithecus afarensis.*
   b. *Australopithecus africanus.*
   c. *Australopithecus aethiopicus.*
   d. *Australopithecus robustus.*

10. The famous "Lucy" fossil was found in
    a. Kenya.
    b. Tanzania.
 * c. Ethiopia.
    d. Uganda.

11. The valgus angle is the angle at which
    a. the spinal column attaches to the base of the skull.
    b. the femur attaches to the pelvis.
 * c. the femur attaches to the knee joint.
    d. the great toe attaches to the bones of the foot.

12. The foramen magnum is
   a.   the hole formed by the pelvic bones that determines the size of the birth canal.
* b.   the hole at the base of the skull through which the spinal cord passes on its way to the brain.
   c.   the space between the zygomatic arch and the skull through which the temporal muscle passes.
   d.   the space between the zygomatic arch and the skull through which the masseter muscle passes.

13. The bones of the fingers and toes of *A. afarensis* are slightly curved, and the toes are much longer than the toes of modern human beings. This suggests to paleoanthropologists that
   a.   the bipedalism of *A. afarensis* was even more efficient than that of modern human beings.
   b.   *A. afarensis* did not move with a full striding gait, as later hominids did.
   c.   *A. afarensis* retained significant tree-climbing ability.
* d.   both b and c

14. The Laetoli footprints
* a.   appear to have been made by a hominid with a striding gait and short, straight toes.
   b.   fit perfectly with the reconstructed foot anatomy of *A. afarensis*.
   c.   were probably made by *Homo habilis*.
   d.   were probably made by *Homo erectus*.

15. Recent finds of *A. Afarensis* from Maka and Hadar
   a.   suggest that all the bones assigned to *A. afarensis* may belong to more than one species.
* b.   appear to confirm the single-species hypothesis.
   c.   suggest that the range of variation of body size in *A. afarensis* is smaller than the range found in any other known species.
   d.   both b and c

16. Which of the following traits does NOT describe the dentition of *A. afarensis?*
   a.   The dental arcade is U-shaped.
* b.   The canines no longer project.
   c.   Some fossil samples show the presence of a diastema.
   d.   The molars are larger than ape molars.

17. Why do some anthropologists believe that *A. afarensis* females preferred to mate with males who were less threatening to themselves and to their offspring?
    a.   They were using hand-made tools instead of teeth in aggressive encounters.
    b.   Their canines were even larger than those of other hominoids.
* c.   Their canines were relatively smaller than those of apes, but they did not make stone tools.
    d.   Females were slightly larger than males.

18. The enormous cheek teeth of the later australopithecines are viewed as an adaptation to
    a.   an exclusively carnivorous diet.
    b.   a diet consisting primarily of fruit and leaves.
    c.   a diet consisting primarily of insects.
* d.   grassland diets consisting of coarse vegetable foods.

19. Those late-australopithecine fossils with enlarged cheek teeth and small, lightly built faces
* a.   are known as gracile australopithecines.
    b.   are known as robust australopithecines.
    c.   include the famous Zinjanthropus fossil.
    d.   both a and c

20. Those late-australopithecine fossils with rugged jaws, flatter faces, truly enormous molars, and a sagittal crest
    a.   are known as gracile australopithecines.
* b.   are known as robust australopithecines.
    c.   include the famous Taung fossil.
    d.   both b and c

21. The hand bones of robust australopithecines
    a.   resemble the hand bones of *A. afarensis*
* b.   look more humanlike than the hand bones of *A. afarensis*
    c.   show evidence of tree-climbing ability.
    d.   both a and c

22. The striking morphological differences between gracile and robust australopithecines
* a.   have to do almost exclusively with their chewing anatomy.
    b.   have to do almost exclusively with their postcranial anatomy.
    c.   are clearest when we compare their cranial capacities.
    d.   are clearest when we compare the thickness of their skull bones.

23. The muscles needed to move the jaws of robust australopithecines are so massive that natural selection seems to have favored the development of a ridge of bone along the midline of the skull for muscle attachment. This is called the
  a.   zygomatic arch.
* b.   sagittal crest.
  c.   diastema.
  d.   parabolic arch.

24. The robust australopithecines, with the largest molars and most massive jaws, also have the flattest faces, due to an enlarged
* a.   zygomatic arch.
  b.   sagittal crest.
  c.   diastema.
  d.   parabolic arch.

25. A mixture of hardened sediments and fossils found in southern African limestone caves
* a.   is called breccia.
  b.   can be dated using potassium-argon methods.
  c.   yielded the famous Zinjanthropus skull.
  d.   both a and c

26. Eastern Africa is unlike southern Africa as a source of hominid fossils because
  a.   in eastern Africa, the fossils lie neatly sandwiched between breccia deposits that can be dated using radiometric methods.
  b.   in southern Africa, the fossils lie neatly sandwiched between datable layers of volcanic rock.
* c.   biostratigraphy from radiometrically dated strata in eastern Africa can be used to date fossils found in southern African breccia deposits.
  d.   biostratigraphy from radiometrically dated strata in southern Africa can be used to date fossils found in eastern African breccia deposits.

27. The "black skull," a 2.5 million years old robust australopithecine fossil found in Koobi Fora, Kenya, in 1985
  a.   shows affinities both to the earlier *A. afarensis* and to the later *A. robustus* and *A. boisei* fossils
  b.   may be ancestral to the later *A. robustus* and *A. boisei* fossils
  c.   suggests an early divergence between robust and gracile australopithecine lineages.
* d.   all of the above

28. The greatest confusion about the gracile hominid lineage
* a.   surrounds those fossils dated to about 2 mya.
   b.   concerns when they diverged from their robust australopithecine ancestors.
   c.   concerns when the robust australopithecines diverged from their gracile australopithecine ancestors.
   d.   both a and b

29. Expansion of the australopithecine brain
   a.   was first noted in the famous Zinjanthropus fossil.
   b.   appears in robust fossils between 4 and 3.5 million years old.
* c.   appears in gracile fossils between 2.5 to 2 million years old.
   d.   was first shown in fossils from southern Africa in the 1960s.

30. In 1963, when Louis Leakey assigned a fossil he had found to a new species called *Homo habilis* he was criticized by other paleontologists because
   a.   the cranial capacity of Leakey's fossil was less than 750 cubic centimeters.
   b.   the cranial capacity of Leakey's fossil was greater than 750 cubic centimeters.
   c.   it did not appear different enough from *A. africanus* or *H. erectus* to merit a separate species designation.
* d.   both a and c

31. The term "morphological space" refers to
   a.   the space between two teeth into which a projecting canine tooth fits when the jaws are closed.
* b.   the degree of anatomical difference separating two different fossil specimens.
   c.   the extent of movement in space made possible by the hominid shoulder joint.
   d.   the space within the pelvic bones that determines the size of the birth canal.

32. Paleoanthropologists suspect that perhaps more than one species belonging to the genus *Homo* may have coexisted in eastern Africa in the early Pleistocene because
* a.   the fossils assigned to *Homo habilis* show too much internal variation to all belong to the same species.
   b.   more than one species of robust australopithecine coexisted in the late Pliocene.
   c.   more than one species of gracile australopithecine has been found in southern Africa.
   d.   both robust and gracile australopithecines coexisted in earlier periods.

33. The key criterion used by paleoanthropologists in deciding whether a gracile fossil younger than 2 million years of age should be placed in the genus *Homo* is
    a.   size of molars.
* b.   cranial capacity.
    c.   presence of a U-shaped dental arcade.
    d.   two premolars instead of three.

34. The australopithecine skull rapidly narrows behind the ridges of bone that form the eye orbits, a morphological feature called the
    a.   foramen magnum.
    b.   valgus angle.
* c.   postorbital constriction.
    d.   zygomatic arch.

35. The cranium of *Homo habilis* lacks a
    a.   foramen magnum.
* b.   postorbital constriction.
    c.   zygomatic arch.
    d.   both b and c

36. Expansion of the brain in *Homo habilis* was NOT accompanied by
* a.   a marked increase in body size.
    b.   thinning of the bones of the skull.
    c.   flattening of the face.
    d.   a more parabolically contoured dental arcade.

37. The oldest undisputed stone tools are at least
    a.   4 million years old.
    b.   3.5 million years old.
    c.   3 million years old.
* d.   2.5 million years old.

38. The style of stone-tool making that involves knocking a few flakes off tennis-ball-sized rocks is called the
    a.   core tradition.
* b.   Oldowan tradition.
    c.   Acheulean tradition.
    d.   chopping tool tradition.

39. The study of the various processes that bones and stones undergo in the course of becoming part of the fossil and archaeological records is called
a. archaeology.
b. paleontology.
c. taphonomy.
d. topography.

40. The oldest undisputed stone tools are said to belong to the
a. core tradition.
b. Oldowan tradition.
c. Acheulean tradition.
d. chopping tool tradition.

41. Whether a stone tool has been used to butcher an animal or to whittle wood can theoretically be determined by
a. examining wear marks along the cutting edge.
b. determining how dull or how sharp the cutting edge is.
c. testing the cutting edge on raw meat and on vegetable fibers in the laboratory.
d. both a and b

42. Taphonomists would probably conclude that hominids had scavenged meat from an animal carcass they did not kill if
a. fossil animal bones showed animal tooth marks on top of stone-tool cutmarks.
b. fossil animal bones showed stone-tool cutmarks on top of animal tooth marks.
c. stone tools and fossil animal bones were found together in the same site.
d. fossil bones showed no sign of weathering.

43. Attempts by anthropologists to replicate ancient stone tools suggest that
a. Oldowan stoneworkers were usually right-handed.
b. Acheulean stoneworkers were usually left-handed.
c. Oldowan stoneworkers were as likely to be right-handed as left-handed.
d. Acheulean stoneworkers were as likely to be right-handed as left-handed.

44. Some anthropologists have claimed that meat eating was the crucial behavioral change leading to the appearance of early *Homo*. This story of human origins is called the

a.   missing link scenario.
* b.   man the hunter scenario.
c.   woman the gatherer scenario.
d.   the foraging scenario.

45. According to Linda Fedigan, the contributors to the volume *Man the Hunter*

a.   provided genetic evidence that the biological bases for killing have been incorporated into human psychology.
b.   were unable to define "hunting" in a consistent manner.
c.   provided recent ethnographic evidence that contemporary "hunters" or "hunter-gatherers" were more dependent on plant food gathered by women than they were on meat hunted by men.
* d.   both b and c

46. Some paleoanthropologists in the 1960s hypothesized that early human society was probably a lot like the society of contemporary savanna baboons. The plausibility of the baboon model rested on

a.   the fact that human beings and baboons are closely related hominoids.
* b.   ecological similarities between the environments to which both groups of primates would have had to adapt.
c.   similarities between population structures in baboon troops and in human societies.
d.   similarities in social organization in baboon troops and in human societies.

47. Some anthropologists objected to modeling early human society on savanna baboons because

* a.   human beings had hominoid ancestors and baboons are Old World monkeys.
b.   the environments to which baboons were adapted was very different from that to which the first hominids would have had to adapt.
c.   they found the society of gelada baboons to be more plausible as a model for early hominid society.
d.   both a and b

48. Anthropologists who favored a chimpanzee model for early human society justified their position on the grounds that
   a.   human beings and chimpanzees are closely related hominoids.
   b.   the first hominids and modern chimpanzees would have had to adapt to ecologically varied habitats.
   c.   chimpanzees use tools and share food with relatives and mates.
 * d.   all of the above

49. Human groups who neither plant crops nor herd animals but rely on a variety of foods that can be collected or caught are called
 * a.   foraging societies.
   b.   horticultural societies.
   c.   pastoral societies.
   d.   transhumant societies.

50. If early human societies are modeled on twentieth-century foraging societies (such as that of the Ju/'hoansi of southern Africa), which of the following features would early human societies have possessed?
   a.   dependency on meat hunted by men for subsistence
   b.   dependency on vegetable foods foraged by women for subsistence
   c.   a flexible form of kinship organization that recognized both the male and the female line
 * d.   both b and c

51. The role women play in food procurement in contemporary foraging societies suggests that a unique skill in the earliest human societies was
   a.   the invention of endurance hunting techniques.
 * b.   the ability of women to arrange their reproductive lives around the demands of their food-gathering activities.
   c.   the ability of men and women to live apart from one another for long periods.
   d.   the ability of active, productive males to provision passive, unproductive females who stayed in base camps to tend offspring.

52. As it has become increasingly clear to paleoanthropologists that human beings are the product of mosaic evolution,
   a.   they are more willing to speak as if a bundle of traits signifying "human nature" originated at one time among our distant ancestors.
 * b.   they are less willing to speak as if a bundle of traits signifying "human nature" originated at one time among our distant ancestors.
   c.   they are increasingly supportive of the "man the hunter" scenario.
   d.   both a and c

53. Which of the following is NOT a typical feature of the skull of *Homo erectus?*
    a.   heavy brow ridges
    b.   a cranial capacity of around 1000 cubic centimeters
    c.   an occipital bun
*   d.   a sagittal crest

54. Basicranial flexion refers to
    a.   the degree of flexibility of movement at the point where the base of the cranium joins the neck.
*   b.   the sharpness of the angle with which the rear surface of the palate arches upward from the front edge of the foramen magnum.
    c.   the degree of flexibility of movement at the point where the femur meets the knee joint.
    d.   the degree of flexibility of movement of the tongue at the point where it attaches to the base of the jaw.

55. Basicranial flexion in *Homo erectus* is less than that of our own species, but greater than that of the australopithecines, which suggests that
    a.   *Homo erectus* could move its head more freely than the australopithecines, but less freely than we do.
*   b.   the throat anatomy of *Homo erectus* was more likely to have been able to produce the speech sounds necessary for human language than was the throat anatomy of the australopithecines.
    c.   the leg anatomy of *Homo erectus* made possible a more efficient form of bipedalism than we ourselves have.
    d.   the leg anatomy of *Homo erectus* made possible a form of bipedalism that was more efficient than that of the australopithecines but less efficient than our own.

56. Wear patterns on the teeth of *Homo erectus*
    a.   are different from those found on *Homo habilis.*
    b.   show heavy pitting and scratching.
    c.   suggest that the diet of *Homo erectus* was significantly different from that of previous hominids.
*   d.   all of the above

57. The postcranial skeleton of *Homo erectus*
    a.   is identical to that of modern human beings.
*   b.   shows a marked reduction in sexual dimorphism compared to earlier hominids.
    c.   shows a greater degree of sexual dimorphism than in earlier hominids.
    d.   both a and c

58. Traditionally, the appearance of *Homo erectus* in the fossil record has been linked with the appearance of a new stone-tool tradition in the archaeological record called
   a.   the Core Tradition.
   b.   the Oldowan Tradition.
* c.   the Acheulean Tradition.
   d.   the Flake Tradition.

59. The Lower Paleolithic in Europe and the Early Stone Age in Africa include
   a.   the Oldowan Tradition.
   b.   the Acheulean Tradition.
   c.   the core Tradition.
* d.   both a and b

60. Paleoanthropologists have found African stone-tool assemblages dating to *Homo erectus* times that contain both Oldowan tools and larger biface tools. They have also found typical Acheulean tools in African sites containing fossils of early *Homo sapiens*. This evidence has led them to conclude that
   a.   *Homo erectus* must have appeared more than 2.5 million years ago.
   b.   *Homo erectus* must have become extinct 100,000 years ago or less.
* c.   more than one hominid species may have made and used tools that we assign to a single archaeological culture.
   d.   both a and b

61. Recent work by taphonomists on sites and remains associated with *Homo erectus* has led them to question
   a.   whether *Homo erectus* hunters killed the animals whose bones have been found together with Acheulean tools.
   b.   whether *Homo erectus* used fire to cook the meat of the animals whose bones have been found in association with *Homo erectus* remains.
   c.   whether *Homo erectus* practiced cannibalism.
* d.   all of the above

62. Binford and Ho argue that
   a.   *Homo erectus* was a hunter who subsisted primarily on cooked meat.
   b.   *Homo erectus* was a cannibal.
   c.   Torralba and Ambrona were sites where *Homo erectus* killed and butchered wild game.
* d.   no good evidence exists to show that *Homo erectus* depended on hunted meat to survive.

63. Some experts who have studied the sites of Torralba and Ambrona
a.   believe that these were "kill sites" showing that *Homo erectus* was a successful big-game hunter.
b.   believe that these sites simply show the remains of predation by large carnivores, rather than by *Homo erectus.*
c.   believe that *Homo sapiens* was responsible for the remains found in these sites.
* d.   both a and b

64. The fossil record for *Homo erectus* impresses supporters of speciation by punctuated equilibrium because
a.   *Homo erectus* fossils found in different geographical regions all seem to possess an instantly recognizable pattern of morphological features.
b.   *Homo erectus* fossils dating to different time periods all seem to possess an instantly recognizable pattern of morphological features.
c.   the fact that *Homo erectus* had changed so little in over a million years of evolution is an example of "stasis", which is important evidence for the punctuated equilibrium model of speciation.
* d.   All of the above are true.

65. Phyletic gradualists believe that the fossil record of *Homo erectus* does not contradict their scenario for speciation because
a.   *Homo erectus* fossils are very hard to find outside of Africa.
b.   *Homo erectus* fossils dating to different time periods show unmistakable, gradual changes in cranial and postcranial morphology.
* c.   a slight increase in cranial capacity from earlier to later *Homo erectus* skulls shows that stasis was not absolute throughout the period when *Homo erectus* walked the earth.
d.   both a and b

Essay Questions

66. What are the four evolutionary changes that occurred during hominid evolution and why is each important?

67. Discuss bipedal locomotion in hominoids. What are the kinds of selective pressures that could have been responsible for its development? What are the major morphological differences between habitual bipedal hominids and occasionally bipedal apes, and what makes the major difference?

68. Why is there disagreement about the status of various australopithecine fossils?

69. What kinds of evidence do paleoanthropologists use for assigning fossils to different hominid genera?

70. Choose one of the theories for the transition from ape to human being and discuss it. What are its basic principles? What are its strengths? Its weaknesses?

71. What is the significance of *Homo erectus* in hominid evolution?

72. Review the evidence for and against *Homo erectus* as a hunter.

CHAPTER 8

THE EVOLUTION OF HOMO SAPIENS

Outline

ARCHAIC *HOMO SAPIENS*

THE NEANDERTALS (130,000–35,000 years ago)

Did Neandertals Speak?

NEANDERTAL CULTURE

Did Neandertals Hunt?

ANATOMICALLY MODERN HUMAN BEINGS (200,000 years ago to present)

MIDDLE STONE AGE CULTURE IN AFRICA

THE UPPER PALEOLITHIC/LATESTONE AGE (40,000? to 12,000 years ago)

THE FATE OF THE NEANDERTALS

UPPER PALEOLITHIC/LATE STONE AGE CULTURE

SPREAD OF MODERN *HOMO SAPIENS* IN LATE PLEISTOCENE TIMES

Eastern Asia and Siberia
The Americas
Australia

TWO MILLION YEARS OF HUMAN EVOLUTION

Key Terms

archaic *Homo sapiens*
out-of-Africa model
regional continuity
    model
anatomically modern
    Homo sapiens
Neandertals
pharynx

Broca's area
Wernicke's area
Mousterian tradition
Middle Paleolithic
Middle Stone Age
intrusions
Howieson's Poort
    Industry

Upper Paleolithic
Late Stone Age
blades
Châtelperronian
    assemblages
Aurignacian assemblages
Paleoindians
Clovis points

Arguing Anthropology

1. What's all the fuss about where the first *Homo sapiens* evolved? Why is it an issue?

2. At the end of this chapter, the authors write, "But one of the knottiest problems that remains concerns how we interpret mounting evidence that human biology and human culture evolved at different rates." Why is this problematic?

Multiple Choice Questions

1. The first hominid species to leave Africa was
   a. *Australopithecus afarensis.*
   b. *Australopithecus africanus.*
   * c. *Homo erectus.*
   d. *Homo sapiens.*

2. The fossils classified as archaic *Homo sapiens* date between
   a. 4 - 3.5 mya.
   b. 3 - 2 mya.
   c. 1.8 mya - 500,000 ya.
   * d. 500,000 - 200,000 ya.

3. Which of the following is NOT a morphological feature of fossils classified as archaic *Homo sapiens*?
   a. massive brow ridges
   * b. chins
   c. broad, vaulted skulls
   d. cranial capacity between 1100 and 1300 cubic centimeters

4. When Günter Bräuer used cladistic methods to compare all the skulls from Africa that had been assigned to archaic *Homo sapiens*, what did he conclude?
   * a. modern *Homo sapiens* evolved from *Homo erectus* only once, in Africa
   b. modern *Homo sapiens* did NOT evolve from African *Homo erectus*
   c. modern *Homo sapiens* probably evolved from Asian *Homo erectus*
   d. the population ancestral to modern *Homo sapiens* cannot be determined

5. According to G. Philip Rightmire, the appearance of modern *Homo sapiens*
    a.   was the result of gradualistic evolution.
    b.   probably occurred in Asia.
*   c.   probably followed the punctuation of an equilibrium that had allowed
            Homo erectus to remain a stable species for over a million years.
    d.   both a and b

6. When archaic *Homo sapiens* appears in the fossil record, what happens to
    the archaeological record?
*   a.   nothing important
    b.   the sudden appearance of Acheulean artifacts
    c.   the sudden appearance of Châtelperronian artifacts
    d.   the sudden appearance of Aurignacian artifacts

7. Which of the following argues that *Homo erectus* is best understood as a
    single, long-lived, geographically dispersed species, one population of
    which, probably in Africa, underwent a rapid spurt of evolution to produce
    Homo sapiens 200,000 to 100,000 years ago?
    a.   the single species model
*   b.   the out-of-Africa model
    c.   the outside-of-Africa model
    d.   the regional continuity model

8. Which of the following argues that *Homo erectus* gradually evolved into
    Homo sapiens throughout the entire traditional range that *Homo erectus*
    occupied?
    a.   the single species model
    b.   the out-of-Africa model
    c.   the outside-of-Africa model
*   d.   the regional continuity model

9. According to Milford Wolpoff, rather isolated populations of *Homo erectus*
    did not evolve into separate species because of
    a.   extinction.
    b.   genetic drift.
*   c.   gene flow.
    d.   mutations.

10. If Milford Wolpoff and his colleagues are correct, the distinct phenotypic features that today distinguish Africans, Asians, and Europeans from one another date back
   a.   2 million years or more.
* b.   1 million years or more.
   c.   about 500,000 years ago.
   d.   about 200,000 years ago.

11. Recent evidence for a 300,000-year-old pre-Neandertal population in Atapuerca, Spain suggests that
* a.   the Neandertal lineage is more ancient than previously considered.
   b.   the Neandertal lineage is younger than previously considered.
   c.   *Homo erectus* probably lived in Europe.
   d.   the ancestors of this population probably came from Asia.

12. Which of the following criticisms has been made of the regional continuity model?
   a.   The fossils being compared are too variable to show any clear patterns of regional resemblance.
   b.   The morphological features supposedly shared by populations of *H. sapiens* and *H. erectus* from the same region are not unique to that region, but are found in *H. erectus* fossils elsewhere, including Africa.
   c.   No fossils showing a transition between *H. erectus* and *H. sapiens* have yet been found.
* d.   all of the above

13. Which of the following criticisms have been made of the out-of-Africa model?
* a.   The mitochondrial DNA analysis that has been taken as independent confirmation of this model were based on faulty calculations.
   b.   The morphological features supposedly shared by populations of *H. sapiens* and *H. erectus* in Africa are not unique to that region but are found in *H. erectus* fossils in Asia.
   c.   no fossils showing a transition between *H. erectus* and *H. sapiens* have yet been found in Africa.
   d.   all of the above

14. Which of the following describes the fossil record for archaic *H. sapiens?*
* a.   It is thin and poorly dated.
   b.   The fewest fossils have been found in Africa.
   c.   Dating is better for Asian specimens than for European or African specimens.
   d.   all of the above

93

15. The "Neandertals" are
a. hominid fossils that apparently evolved from an earlier population of *Homo erectus* in Africa about 500,000 years ago.
* b. hominid fossils from Europe and western Asia that apparently evolved from an earlier population of archaic *Homo sapiens* about 130,000 years ago.
c. hominid fossils from China that apparently evolved from an earlier population of *Homo erectus* about 1 million years ago.
d. hominid fossils from Asia that apparently evolved from an earlier population of archaic *Homo sapiens* about 200,000 years ago.

16. Which of the following does NOT describe Neandertal morphology?
a. more robust than modern *Homo sapiens*
b. taurodontism
* c. chins
d. retromolar spaces

17. The average Neandertal cranial capacity
* a. is larger than that of modern human populations.
b. is smaller than that of modern human populations.
c. averages about 1400 cubic centimeters.
d. suggests that the Neandertal brain was symmetrical.

18. The muscle-walled space between the larynx and the soft palate is known as
a. the voice box.
* b. the pharynx.
c. the vocal tract.
d. the speech canal.

19. Which of the following describes the throat anatomy of modern human beings?
* a. The larynx is located low in the neck.
b. The larynx is located high in the neck.
c. The basicranium is relatively flat.
d. The pharynx is tiny.

20. Which of the following describes the throat anatomy of Neandertals?
a. The larynx is located lower in the neck than in modern human beings.
* b. The basicranium is relatively flat.
c. The basicranium is flexed as fully as it is in modern human beings.
d. both a and b

21. According to Jeffrey Laitman, which best describes the probable linguistic abilities of the Neandertals?
   a.   They possessed a fully-developed form of language-as-we-know-it.
   b.   They could produce about the same range of sounds as *Homo habilis.*
 * c.   They probably had a more restricted vocal range than modern adult human beings.
   d.   They probably had a greater vocal range than modern adult human beings.

22. That portion of the brain that controls speech production is called
 * a.   Broca's area.
   b.   Lieberman's area.
   c.   Laitman's area.
   d.   Wernicke's area.

23. That portion of the brain that controls speech interpretation is called
   a.   Broca's area.
   b.   Lieberman's area.
   c.   Laitman's area.
 * d.   Wernicke's area.

24. Associated with Neandertal finds in Europe and southwestern Asia is a new stone-tool tradition called the
   a.   Acheulean.
 * b.   Mousterian.
   c.   Aurignacian.
   d.   Châtelperronian.

25. Flake tools produced by the Levallois technique are characteristic of which stone-tool tradition?
   a.   Acheulean
 * b.   Mousterian
   c.   Aurignacian
   d.   Châtelperronian

26. The Middle Paleolithic in Europe and the Middle Stone Age in Africa are indicated by which of the following stone-tool traditions?
   a.   Acheulean
 * b.   Mousterian
   c.   Aurignacian
   d.   Châtelperronian

27. The earliest Middle Stone Age tools in Africa are probably about how old?
  a.   2.5 million years old
  b.   1.8 million years old
  c.   800,000 years old
* d.   200,000 years old

28. The earliest hominid sites in the European part of the former Soviet Union
  a.   contain Mousterian tools.
  b.   contain Châtelperronian tools.
  c.   suggest that Neandertals were the first hominids capable of settling in areas with such a cold, harsh climate.
* d.   both a and c

29. Which of the following is NOT an explanation for differences in the numbers and kinds of tools in Mousterian assemblages?
  a.   These differences reflect the cultural differences of their makers.
* b.   These differences reflect the fact that different hominid species were making Mousterian tools.
  c.   These differences reflect seasonal toolkits for a single group of people.
  d.   These differences reflect different stages in the life of a tool as it is periodically resharpened before being discarded.

30. Artifacts made by more recent populations that accidentally find their way into lower geological strata as the result of natural forces are called
  a.   anachronisms.
  b.   chronotopes.
  c.   red herrings.
* d.   intrusions.

31. Which of the following statements describes Neandertal culture?
* a.   They buried their dead.
  b.   They left a profusion of objects made of bone, ivory, antler, and shell.
  c.   Many of their dwellings have been excavated.
  d.   all of the above

32. According to taphonomists such as Richard Klein, the best evidence for Neandertal "humanity" is the fact that
  a.   they buried their dead.
  b.   they made a profusion of objects out of bone, ivory, antler, and shell.
* c.   they cared for the old and sick.
  d.   they worshipped the cave bear.

33. Evidence for Neandertal hunting
a.   is often difficult to determine.
b.   includes a wooden spear found lying under the carcass of an elephant that dates to the period when Neandertals were the only hominids in Europe.
c.   suggests that their diet does not seem to have differed much from that of the modern people who replaced them.
* d.   all of the above

34. Compared to Neandertals, anatomically modern human beings
* a.   are less robust.
b.   have larger molars.
c.   have retromolar spaces.
d.   both b and c

35. Anatomically modern human fossils from Klasies River Mouth Cave in South Africa
a.   came from deposits beyond the range of radiocarbon dating.
b.   were cross-dated using paleoclimatic and biostratigraphic methods.
c.   were cross-dated using uranium-series dating and electron-spin resonance.
* d.   all of the above

36. Anatomically modern human fossils from Klasies River Mouth Cave
a.   are between 100,000 and 200,000 years old.
b.   are between 75,000 and 100,000 years old.
* c.   are between 60,000 and 74,000 years old.
d.   are between 40,000 and 24,000 years old.

37. Anatomically modern human fossils from Qafzeh Cave in Israel
a.   were dated using the radiocarbon method.
* b.   lived about 92,000 years ago.
c.   were descendants of Neandertals from southwestern Asia.
d.   both b and c

38. Traditionally, many paleoanthropologists thought that anatomically modern people descended from Neandertals because
a.   they thought modern people first appeared about 40,000 years ago.
b.   they thought Neandertals died out about 40,000 years ago.
c.   they lacked evidence about the origins of modern humans from outside of Europe.
* d.   all of the above

39. In the 1930s, hominid fossils from Skhul were interpreted as
a.   evidence of interbreeding between anatomically modern and Neandertal populations.
* b.   evidence of the evolutionary transition between Neandertals and anatomically modern humans.
c.   makers of Aurignacian tools.
d.   makers of Châatelperronian tools.

40. The Neandertal burial at Kebara Cave has been dated by thermoluminescence to about
a.   200,000 years ago.
b.   100,000 years ago.
c.   92,000 years ago.
* d.   60,000 years ago.

41. Neandertal remains from Tabun and modern human remains from Qafzeh
a.   are associated with different stone tool traditions.
b.   are associated with different burial patterns.
* c.   are both associated with Mousterian culture.
d.   are both associated with Aurignacian culture.

42. Tools and other cultural remains from southwestern Asian sites indicate that
a.   Neandertals made Mousterian tools and modern humans made Aurignacian tools.
b.   Neandertals lived in caves and modern humans lived in outdoor sites.
c.   Neandertals and modern humans lived in the same sites, but at different times.
* d.   Neandertals and modern humans both participated in Mousterian culture.

43. Remains of mollusk shells and bones of fur seals and penguins found at Klasies River Mouth Cave, and dating to Middle Stone Age times, suggest to Richard Klein that
a.   Neandertals probably used these animals for food.
b.   Anatomically modern people did not use the site.
* c.   Middle Stone Age people had not mastered skills connected with fishing and fowling.
d.   both a and b

44. The Howieson's Poort Industry is an unusual Middle Stone Age industry because
a.   it has been dated to Late Stone Age times.
b.   it contains flakes made by the Levallois technique.
c.   it contains bone fishhooks and stone net- or line-sinkers.
* d.   it includes a number of backed tools that look like Late Stone Age blades.

45. The Upper Paleolithic/Late Stone Age lasted from about
a.   400,000 to 130,000 years ago.
b.   130,000 to 40,000 years ago.
* c.   40,000 to 12,000 years ago.
d.   12,000 to 8,000 years ago.

46. The typical Upper Paleolithic/Late Stone Age tool is
a.   the prismatic core.
* b.   the blade.
c.   the bone fishhook.
d.   the denticulate.

47. The site of Boker Tachtit in the Negev Desert of Israel is important because
a.   it yielded bones of anatomically modern humans that were 92,000 years old.
b.   it yielded bones of Neandertals that were 105,000 years old.
* c.   it yielded a series of levels in which Mousterian/Middle Stone Age flake technology is gradually replaced by Upper Paleolithic/Late Stone Age blade technology.
d.   it yielded a series of levels in which Mousterian/Middle Stone Age flake technology is found above Upper Paleolithic/Late Stone Age blade technology.

48. Mousterian/Middle Stone Age tool traditions and Upper Paleolithic/Late Stone Age tool traditions are DIFFERENT because
* a.   the Mousterian/Middle Stone Age tradition persists for more than 100,000 years with little change, whereas several different Upper Paleolithic/Late Stone Age tool traditions replace one another in just 20,000 years.
b.   anatomically modern people did not use Mousterian/Middle Stone Age tools, whereas they did use Upper Paleolithic/Late Stone Age tools.
c.   Mousterian/Middle Stone Age traditions typically involve blades, whereas Upper Paleolithic/Late Stone Age traditions typically involve flakes.
d.   Mousterian/Middle Stone Age toolmakers did not know the Levallois technique of core preparation, whereas Upper Paleolithic/Late Stone Age toolmakers did.

49. The transition between Mousterian/Middle Stone Age and Upper
    Paleolithic/Late stone age traditions
    a.   is gradual, with Mousterian/MSA flakes slowly being transformed into
            Upper Paleolithic/LSA blades.
    b.   is gradual, with Mousterian/MSA blades slowly being transformed into
            Upper Paleolithic/LSA flakes.
*   c.   is striking, with Mousterian/MSA tools being replaced by far more
            elaborate artifacts in the Upper Paleolithic/LSA.
    d.   has never been documented in an archaeological excavation.

50. Châtelperronian assemblages
*   a.   date from about 35,000 to 30,000 years ago.
    b.   contain typical Mousterian blades.
    c.   mark the appearance of Neandertals in Europe.
    d.   both b and c

51. Aurignacian assemblages
*   a.   date from about 34,000 to 30,000 years ago.
    b.   are typical Mousterian assemblages.
    c.   mark the appearance of Neandertals in Europe.
    d.   both b and c

52. Which of the following assemblages contains a mixture of burins, bone
    tools, pierced animal teeth, and typical Mousterian backed knives?
    a.   Acheulean
    b.   Aurignacian
*   c.   Châtelperronian
    d.   Gravettian

53. Which of the following assemblages is thought by some
    paleoanthropologists to be evidence for a gradual transition between Lower
    and Upper Paleolithic cultures?
    a.   Acheulean
    b.   Aurignacian
*   c.   Châtelperronian
    d.   Gravettian

54. The controversy concerning the Châtelperronian assemblage concerns
    a.   whether Neandertals could have made Châtelperronian tools.
    b.   whether Neandertals invented blade technology as they evolved into
            anatomically modern human beings.
    c.   whether the Neandertals borrowed elements of Upper Paleolithic blade
            technology from a culturally more advanced population of outsiders.
*   d.   both b and c

55. Deposits found in some cave sites in southwestern France and northern Spain are important to the Châtelperronian controversy because

* a.   they show some Châtelperronian layers on top of some Aurignacian layers.

b.   they show some Aurignacian layers on top of some Châtelperronian layers.

c.   they show Neandertals in association with Aurignacian tools.

d.   they show Neandertals in association with Gravettian tools.

56. Analysis of pollen and sediments from different Aurignacian sites suggest that

* a.   Aurignacian peoples first appeared in southern France and then spread northward.

b.   Gravettian peoples arrived in southern France before the Aurignacians.

c.   Aurignacian peoples migrated from eastern Europe, bringing domesticated plants with them.

d.   A single group of people used Aurignacian tools in the summer and Châtelperronian tools in the winter.

57. A number of experts have concluded that

* a.   anatomically modern people invented the Aurignacian industry in southwestern Asia and brought it with them when they migrated into central and western Europe.

b.   Neandertals invented the Aurignacian industry in eastern Europe and brought it with them when they migrated into central and western Europe.

c.   anatomically modern people invented the Aurignacian industry in eastern Europe and brought it with them when they migrated into central and western Europe.

d.   anatomically modern people invented the Aurignacian industry in eastern Europe and brought it with them when they migrated into southwestern Asia.

58. Anthropologists generally reject the notion that invading modern people exterminated the Neandertals because

a.   most of them believe that Neandertals could have defended themselves against invaders.

* b.   there is no evidence to suggest that the replacement of Neandertals by modern people was anything other than peaceful.

c.   modern people did not possess weapons until long after the Neandertals were extinct.

d.   both b and c

59. Some anthropologists do not believe that Neandertals and modern people regularly interbred because
a.   Neandertals and modern people lived side by side in southwestern Asia for 45,000 years without losing their phenotypic distinctiveness.
b.   some cladistic analyses suggest that modern Europeans share no derived morphological traits with the Neandertals.
c.   the Neandertal gestation period was several months longer than the gestation period of modern humans.
* d.   both a and b

60. Brian Fagan calls the technological explosion of Upper Paleolithic/Late Stone Age material culture the "Swiss army knife effect" because
a.   Upper Paleolithic people carried several different blades together on a leather thong, like a Swiss army knife.
* b.   the flexible core and blade technique allowed Upper Paleolithic/LSA stoneworkers to develop a variety of subsidiary crafts.
c.   stone blades were used to work bone and antler into tools which were carried together on a leather thong, like a Swiss army knife.
d.   the best, most complete assemblages of Upper Paleolithic tools have been found in Switzerland.

61. Which of the following was part of Upper Paleolithic/LSA culture?
a.   bows and arrows
b.   tailored clothing
c.   bone harpoons
* d.   all of the above

62. The most striking evidence for a modern human capacity for culture in the Upper Paleolithic/LSA comes from
a.   deliberate burials.
b.   regular hunting of large game.
* c.   art.
d.   domesticated plants.

63. Modern human beings in the Upper Paleolithic/LSA
a.   were more numerous and more widespread than were previous hominids.
b.   suffered few injuries and were relatively healthy.
c.   were the first hominids to occupy the coldest, harshest climates in Asia.
* d.   all of the above

64. Clovis points were made by
* a.   Paleoindians.
  b.   Aurignacians.
  c.   Neandertals.
  d.   Australians.

65. The least controversial date for the peopling of the Americas is
* a.   about 12,000 years ago.
  b.   about 18,000 years ago.
  c.   about 33,000 years ago.
  d.   about 40,000 years ago.

66. Modern people first arrived in Australia
  a.   about 12,000 years ago.
  b.   about 18,000 years ago.
  c.   about 33,000 years ago.
* d.   about 40,000 years ago.

67. The peopling of the Americas and of Australia by modern human beings
  a.   took place about 33,000 years ago.
* b.   is connected to widespread extinctions of wild game on both
              continents.
  c.   occurred after the domestication of plants and animals.
  d.   required migrating through ice-free corridors to the south.

Essay Questions

68. Compare and contrast the "Out-of-Africa" and regional continuity models for the evolution from *Homo erectus* to *Homo sapiens*. What kinds of evidence is used for each model? What kinds of contrasting interpretations are given for the same evidence?

69. What separates Neandertals from anatomically modern human beings? in your answer use data from at least two of the following: morphology, language, and culture.

70. Summarize the evidence for the fate of the Neandertals.

71. Why is the study of stone tools so important for the study of human evolution?

CHAPTER 9

AFTER THE ICE AGE: SEDENTISM, DOMESTICATION, AND AGRICULTURE

Outline

THE END OF THE PALEOLITHIC AND THE END OF SEDENTISM

PLANT DOMESTICATION

ANIMAL DOMESTICATION

THE MOTOR OF DOMESTICATION

Population Arguments
Climate Arguments
Famine Arguments
The Broad Spectrum Foraging Argument
The Marginal Zone Argument
Conflict Arguments
Multiple Strand Theories

DOMESTICATION IN PRACTICE

Natufian Sedentism
Natufian Social Organization
Natufian Subsistence
Natufians, Climate, and Cultivation
The First Domesticated Plants
Domestication Elsewhere in the World

THE CONSEQUENCES OF DOMESTICATION AND SEDENTISM

"Our Land"
Fertility, Sedentism, and Diet
The Decline in the Quality of the Diet
Increase in Insecurity
Environmental Degradation
Increase in Labor

WHY AGRICULTURE?

Reliability of the Food Supply
Opportunity for Social Complexity

Key Terms

sedentism	broad spectrum foraging	chiefdom
domestication	Natufian tradition	Neolithic
agriculture	social stratification	monocropping

Arguing Anthropology

1. Was agriculture really "the worst mistake in the history of the human race"?

2. What are the drawbacks of a foraging way of life?

Multiple Choice Questions

1. The Pleistocene ended about how many years ago?
* a.   10,000
  b.   25,000
  c.   40,000
  d.   75,000

2. Which of the following was NOT a transformation of the earth's climate at the end of the Pleistocene?
  a.   shifts in the winds that brought moisture-bearing clouds
* b.   declining sea levels
  c.   changes in environments
  d.   all of the above

3. The process of increasingly permanent human habitation in one place is called
  a.   agriculture.
  b.   domestication.
* c.   sedentism.
  d.   urbanization.

4. sedentism:nomadism::
  a.   agriculture:hunting
* b.   staying put:wandering
  c.   transforming animals:transforming plants
  d.   hunting:gathering

5. Human interference with the reproduction of another species, making the species more useful to people is called
  a.   agriculture.
* b.   domestication.
  c.   sedentism.
  d.   urbanization.

6. The systematic modification of the environments of plants and animals to increase their productivity and usefulness is called
* a.   agriculture.
  b.   domestication.
  c.   sedentism.
  d.   urbanization.

7. David Rindos argues that plant domestication came about because
* a.   there were natural selection effects on the plants based on the unconscious activities of people in eating and propagating the plants.
  b.   people intervened directly in the fields, selecting the largest and tastiest seeds to preserve and plant.
  c.   of a combination of environmental and nutritional factors that favored the development of human interest in modifying the plants they ate.
  d.   only those plants that were most attractive to human beings survived after human beings began eating plants.

8. A conflict among scholars concerning domestication centers around
* a.   whether people were aware of what they were doing in intervening in the gene pool of wild plants.
  b.   how plants could have evolved to meet the needs of the people who were eating them.
  c.   whether women or men were the domesticators of plants.
  d.   how people were able to domesticate plants and animals at the same time.

9. To be dispersed successfully in its wild state, wheat requires
* a.   a brittle rachis.
  b.   a soft glume.
  c.   a large seed head.
  d.   seeds that mature at the same time.

10. Compared to wild wheat, domesticated wheat
  a.   is better tasting.
  b.   has a larger seed head.
  c.   has six rows of kernels rather than two.
* d.   all of the above

11. Which of the following is not one of the major food-yielding systems?
  a.   agriculture
  b.   cultivation
* c.   wild-plant-food development
  d.   wild-plant-food production

12. According to the text, animal domestication differed from plant domestication in which of the following ways
* a.   Animal domestication required active human intervention.
  b.   The processes are not different.
  c.   Animal domestication required less precise temperature control than did plant domestication.
  d.   Plant domestication required intervening in the gene pool of the plants.

13. Which of the following is NOT evidence for animal domestication?
  a.   abrupt population increase of some species relative to others
  b.   morphological changes in animal populations
* c.   absence of animal species outside its natural range
  d.   remains of juvenile animals at a site

14. Why is the discovery of remains of many immature male herd animals at a site taken as evidence of human involvement with a herd?
  a.   Hunters kill animals they find; they do not go out of their way to kill only young males.
  b.   Only a small number of males are required for reproduction in a managed herd.
  c.   Hunters are likely to kill the animals easiest to hunt; immature wild male herd animals are always on the outskirts of the herd.
* d.   both a and b

15. Which of the following characteristics is NOT desirable in an animal if domestication is the goal?
  a.   suitable for food
  b.   multiple uses for human beings
  c.   herd animal
* d.   difficult to control

16. The earliest evidence for goat herding is about
  a.   7,000 years ago.
* b.   11,000 years ago.
  c.   15,000 years ago.
  d.   21,000 years ago.

17. The stage in human-animal relationships that is characterized by selective hunting of herds is called
  a.   random hunting.
* b.   controlled hunting.
  c.   herd following.
  d.   loose herding.

18. The stage in human-animal relationships in which people begin to control the movements of a herd is called
    a.   controlled hunting.
    b.   herd following.
*   c.   loose herding.
    d.   close herding.

19. Richard Meadow argues herding represents a complete change in human attitudes toward and relationships with animals. Why?
    a.   Animals are no longer for eating, they are for herding.
*   b.   The focus shifts from the hunted animal to the offspring.
    c.   The focus shifts from meat to animal byproducts, especially milk and hides.
    d.   Animals become the objects of affection rather than fear.

20. Which of the following is NOT a theory for the cause of domestication?
    a.   broad-spectrum foraging
    b.   climatic changes
*   c.   independent invention
    d.   population pressure

21. A population is living off a secure subsistence base, eating plants and animals caught by hunting, fishing, and gathering. The population expands, and as it does, it puts pressure on the resource base, forcing people to eat "third-choice" foods, especially grains. They discovered that the grain responded to human efforts to increase yields and came to rely increasingly on it. This scenario would fit best with which of the following theories of agricultural development?
*   a.   broad-spectrum foraging theory
    b.   conflict theory
    c.   marginal zone theory
    d.   population pressure

22. A modern multiple strand theory of domestication will include the local effects of
    a.   climate.
    b.   environment.
    c.   social organization.
*   d.   all of the above

23. The first evidence of the cultural tradition called the Natufian is found at about how many years before the present?
 a. 8,000
 b. 10,300
 c. 12,500
 d. 15,500

24. Which of the following is evidence that the Natufians lived in relatively permanent settlements?
 a. There are bones of young gazelles and migratory birds at the sites.
 b. There are permanent buildings at settlement sites.
 c. There are cemeteries.
 d. all of the above

25. According to the text, both Belfer-Cohen and Henry argue that extensive Natufian artistic activity was connected with
 a. burial activities.
 b. handling social tensions.
 c. hunting magic.
 d. trade.

26. The evidence from Natufian burials leads scholars like Donald Henry to conclude that
 a. the Natufians maintained an egalitarian social organization.
 b. infectious disease affected Natufian social organization once they became sedentary.
 c. there was unequal access to wealth, power, and prestige in Natufian society.
 d. the Natufians were an early example of a society of consumption.

27. How did the Natufians respond to the changes in the resources they depended on?
 a. Some began to keep cereal plants growing in areas that were no longer ideal.
 b. Some returned to a nomadic foraging way of life.
 c. Some moved into what is now Egypt.
 d. both a and b

28. The appearance of domesticated plants is taken to be the end of one great cultural period and the beginning of another. The period that ends with the beginning of domestication is called the
   a.   Neolithic.
   b.   Natufian.
 * c.   Paleolithic.
   d.   Premodern.

29. The culture in which the agricultural subsistence strategy expanded rapidly was the
   a.   Anatolian.
   b.   Natufian.
   c.   PPNA.
 * d.   PPNB.

30. In the New World, which of the following appeared together?
 * a.   beans, squash, maize
   b.   beans, squash, peppers
   c.   garlic, peppers, maize
   d.   squash, maize, potatoes

31. Which of the following is a consequence of domestication?
   a.   decline in quality of diet
   b.   reliance on smaller number of plants
   c.   environmental degradation
 * d.   all of the above

32. According to the text, how do sedentism and domestication represent a change in worldview?
   a.   People are more aware of the value of the natural environment.
 * b.   Land is transformed into owned territories.
   c.   Plants and animals become objects of worship.
   d.   all of the above

33. Which of the following is NOT an effect of sedentism on fertility?
   a.   Child-spacing intervals decrease with sedentism.
 * b.   Fertility rates decline with sedentism.
   c.   The energy drain on women declines with sedentism.
   d.   Infant and child mortality rates decline with sedentism.

34. The production of prolactin in women
   a.   suppresses ovulation.
   b.   is stimulated by frequent breastfeeding of children.
   c.   is stimulated by endurance exercise.
 * d.   both a and b

35. A diet increasingly rich in cereals would have
 * a.   lowered the ratio of protein to carbohydrate in the diet.
   b.   decreased women's positive energy balance.
   c.   led to lowered fat levels in fertile women.
   d.   all of the above

36. With regard to diet,
   a.   foragers did not eat as well as early farmers.
   b.   foragers and early farmers differed only in the amount of animal
            protein in their diets.
 * c.   early farmers did not eat as well as foragers.
   d.   neither early farmers nor foragers ate very well.

37. Why did the overall insecurity of the food supply system increase as
    dependency on domesticated crops increased?
   a.   A reliance on a smaller number of plants increases the risk if they fail.
   b.   Selective breeding decreases the variability of the plant's gene pool.
   c.   People came increasingly to depend on forces beyond their control—
            hail, rain, pests—that could wipe out the food supply.
 * d.   all of the above

38. Monocropping is the process of
   a.   growing one kind of plant per year.
 * b.   growing one kind of plant per field.
   c.   growing one crop per year.
   d.   all of the above

39. Monocropping increases efficiency and short-term yield. It also
 * a.   exposes the entire field to destruction by disease or pest damage.
   c.   increases the variability of the plant gene pool.
   d.   makes it more difficult to support a growing population.
   b.   reduces the amount of work women must do in the fields.

40. Which of the following is NOT a reason for the increase in disease
    following sedentism and the rise of domestication?
   a.   problems with the disposal of human waste
   b.   people could no longer walk away from disease
 * c.   problems with the distance to fields from settlements
   d.   both a and b

41. Which of the following is an advantage of agriculture?
    a.   extraction of great amounts of energy
    b.   predictable food supply
    c.   reduction in disease
  * d.   both a and b

42. foraging:domestication::
  * a.   reliability:predictability
    b.   simplicity:complexity
    c.   variation:valuation
    d.   all of the above

Essay Questions

43. What are the differences among sedentism, domestication, and agriculture? Provide examples of each and explain why each is important.

44. Discuss two or three of the human-plant relationships discussed in the text. Be sure to indicate the significance of each and the energy balance of each.

45. Choose two or three explanations for the transition to domestication. What are the major points of each? What are the problems with each? Explain the importance of each explanation.

46. Using the Natufians as an example, discuss the multiple strands that seem to have led them to domestication.

47. Discuss fertility and sedentism and domestication.

48. What is the connection of agriculture and disease?

49. Jared Diamond contends that "agriculture was the biggest mistake in human history." What would lead him to conclude that?

50. Compare and contrast foraging and agriculture in terms of the relationship of people to the food supply.

CHAPTER 10

THE EVOLUTION OF COMPLEX SOCIETIES

Outline

ARCHAEOLOGICAL EVIDENCE FOR SOCIAL COMPLEXITY

CATEGORIES OF SOCIAL ORGANIZATION

A NOTE ABOUT POTTERY AND WRITING

Pottery
Writing

HOW CAN ANTHROPOLOGISTS EXPLAIN THE RISE OF COMPLEX
    SOCIETIES?

Mesopotamian Civilization
Andean Civilization

Key Terms

egalitarian societies
social stratification
social complexity
surplus production
occupational
    specialization
social class
monumental architecture

burials
concentrations of
    particular artifacts
band
tribe
rank society
chiefdom
state

empire
cultural horizon
civilization
stamp seals/cylinder
    seals
vertical archipelago
system

Arguing Anthropology

1. To what degree are inequality and violence a fundamental part of the social
    system of the state?

2. The reasons for the emergence of the state as a form of social organization
    are still not clear. What do you think prompted this change in human social
    organization?

Multiple Choice Questions

1. In what kind of society are you likely to find no great differences in wealth,
    power, or prestige among people?
    a.   egalitarian
    b.   modern
    c.   state
    d.   stratified

2. According to the text, societies based on the assumption that different groups in society are entitled to different amounts of wealth, power, and prestige are called
   a. advanced.
   b. egalitarian.
   c. foraging.
 * d. stratified.

3. Which of the following contributed to the evolution of social stratification?
   a. occupational specialization
   b. settled life
   c. surplus production of food
 * d. all of the above

4. In the text, complex societies are distinguished from foraging societies on the basis of
   a. mental level.
   b. social organization.
   c. technology.
 * d. both b and c

5. Which of the following areas did NOT give rise to one of the first states?
   a. China
 * b. Europe
   c. Indus Valley
   d. Mesoamerica

6. Which of the following is archaeological evidence for social complexity?
   a. burials
 * b. monumental architecture
   c. permanent settlements
   d. tools

7. Which of the following is NOT a form of monumental architecture?
 * a. farm house
   b. palace
   c. royal tomb
   d. temple

8. Archaeologists digging at a site in southwest Asia find a series of burials that differ in size, construction, and the quantity of objects found in each. The archaeologists might conclude that the society responsible for the burials was
   a.   egalitarian.
* b.   stratified.
   c.   unequal.
   d.   both b and c

9. It has been suggested that the massive expenditure of resources by early elites was a
   a.   motor for trade.
   b.   tribute to their leadership offered by the "ordinary people" of the society.
   c.   way of consolidating power by forcing possible enemies to work for them.
* d.   way of demonstrating the superior power of the rulers.

10. Which of the following is NOT a category of human societies to which archaeologists ordinarily assign assemblages?
   a.   band
   b.   state
   c.   tribe
* d.   village

11. The characteristic form of social organization among foragers is the
* a.   band.
   b.   chiefdom.
   c.   tribe.
   d.   state.

12. In bands, labor is usually divided by
   a.   age and sex.
   b.   occupation.
   c.   location.
   d.   family.

13. In a rank society, a chief is given greater
   a.   prestige than other people, but not greater power or wealth.
   b.   prestige and wealth than other people, but not greater power.
   c.   wealth and power than other people, but not greater prestige.
   d.   wealth than other people, but not greater prestige and power.

14. A society in which one person and his relatives have privileged access to wealth, power, and prestige is called a
    a.   band.
*   b.   chiefdom.
    c.   rank society.
    d.   tribe.

15. Which of the following is characteristic of a state?
    a.   a stratified society
    b.   possesses a territory
    c.   institutions to collect taxes
*   d.   all of the above

16. When archaeologists find unique styles in architecture, pottery, textiles, and other artifacts distributed uniformly over a wide area, they call this a/an
*   a.   cultural horizon.
    b.   imperial vista.
    c.   state.
    d.   stratified society.

17. Why has pottery been important to archaeological reconstruction?
    a.   Many archaeologists have a background in pottery.
    b.   The development of pottery in an area is shaped by the gender relations in the area.
*   c.   Pottery styles can be used as a form of relative dating.
    d.   All of the above are true.

18. The earliest writing systems were based on drawings of the objects being represented, called
    a.   logograms.
*   b.   pictograms.
    c.   syllabic script.
    d   telegrams.

19. When scribes started using signs to represent sounds rather than meanings, the writing system they invented is called
    a.   telegraphic.
    b.   logographic.
    c.   pictographic.
*   d.   syllabic.

20. The major advantage of an alphabetic writing system over other writing systems is that
a.   better records can be kept.
* b.   fewer signs need to be learned.
c.   more complex ideas can be represented.
d.   both a and b

21. Which of the following ancient civilizations had no writing system?
a.   Chinese
b.   Harappan
* c.   Inca
d.   Maya

22. Which of the following has been an explanation proposed for the rise of complex societies?
a.   The need to contruct and maintain irrigation systems in dry regions arose.
b.   Population pressure required someone to exercise power to allocate resources and keep social chaos from erupting.
c.   Sedentary life in farming villages gave people the leisure time to invent social and technological complexity.
* d.   All of the above are true.

23. Robert Carneiro's theory of environmental circumscription holds that
a.   the environments in the areas where social complexity began are particularly suitable for agriculture, providing the surplus required.
* b.   when hostile environments halt village expansion, new farmland could only be taken from other villages by force.
c.   when environments changed due to climatic changes, the only way for people to survive was to grant the chief greater power.
d.   the need to defend lands with favorable environmental circumstances led to the emergence of an elite.

24. Sociocultural features that have been suggested as leading to the rise of social complexity include
a.   the presence of chiefdoms in the areas in which social complexity first began.
b.   ineffective patterns of conflict resolution within the original social organization.
c.   the innate human need to control others.
d.   both a and b

25. The main difficulty faced by theories that attempt to explain the origins of social complexity in terms of social relations, political culture, or religious beliefs is that
* a.   such phenomena leave no clear traces in the archaeological record.
  b.   the record of these phenomena in the archaeological record can be interpreted in several different ways.
  c.   they ignore environmental factors.
  d.   both a and c

26. Where is the "Fertile Crescent"?
  a.   the Indus River valley in India
  b.   the Mississippi River valley in present-day Minnesota and Iowa
* c.   southwestern Asia, especially the Tigris and Euphrates River valley
  d.   the South American coast in present-day Peru

27. The first states appeared in Mesopotamia about how many years ago?
  a.   2,750
  b.   3,500
* c.   5,000
  d.   6,500

28. Which of the following features was responsible for the development of social complexity in Mesopotamia?
  a.   irrigation agriculture under bureaucratic control
  b.   warfare
  c.   population pressure
* d.   none of the above

29. Which of the following is NOT an Andean society of the pre-Spanish conquest period?
  a.   Chavín
* b.   Mole
  c.   Tiwanaku
  d.   Wari

30. The rise of the Inca state dates to about
  a.   375 B.C.
  b.   1235 A.D.
* c.   1445 A.D.
  d.   1525 A.D.

31. The distinctive Andean pattern of integrating economic resources from a variety of environments is called the
a.   environmental circumscription system.
b.   late intermediate period.
c.   local option system.
d.   vertical archipelago system.

32. The period of Inca dominance is known as
a.   early horizon.
b.   early intermediate period.
c.   late horizon.
d.   middle horizon.

Essay Questions

33. Compare and contrast tribes and chiefdoms with reference to stratification.

34. What are the bases for the rise of social complexity?

35. Explain the ways in which architecture can be used as a way for archaeologists to gauge social complexity.

36. Choose two or three of the explanations offered for the rise of social complexity. Describe how each accounts for the development of social complexity. What are the limitations of each theory? Does one seem more convincing to you? Why?

37. What similarities do you see between the rise of social complexity in Mesopotamia and the Andes?

CHAPTER 11

CULTURE AND THE HUMAN CONDITION

Outline

THE HUMAN CONDITION AND CULTURE

HOLISM

CULTURAL DIFFERENCES

Ethnocentrism
The Cross-Cultural Relationship
Cultural Relativism

CULTURE, HISTORY, AND HUMAN AGENCY

THE PROMISE OF THE ANTHROPOLOGICAL PERSPECTIVE

Key Terms

culture	materialism	dialectical relationships
symbol	reductionism	ethnocentrism
dualsim	determinism	cultural relativism
idealism	holism	

Arguing Anthropology

1. At the time this question is being written, Hutus and Tutsi are slaughtering each other in Rwanda. Can cultural relativism help explain why this is happening and why the French have sent military forces to that country?

2. What is the human condition in the world? What does it mean to be a human being?

Multiple Choice Questions

1. The human condition is distinguished from the condition of other living species by
* a.   culture.
   b.   learning.
   c.   nature.
   d.   openness.

2. Culture is
a.   learned.
b.   shared.
c.   symbolic.
d.   all of the above

3. _____ is the philosophical position that reality consists of two equal and irreducible forces.
a.   Idealism
b.   Rationalism
c.   Materialism
d.   Dualism

4. The claim that human behavior ultimately depends on what human beings think or believe is called
a.   dualism.
b.   idealism.
c.   materialism.
d.   ethnocentrism.

5. The claim that ideas, or the human mind that produces them, is the essence of human nature is called
a.   environmental determinism.
b.   historical materialism.
c.   idealism.
d.   none of the above

6. Views of human nature that ascribe primary importance to our physical makeup are referred to as
a.   materialistic.
b.   idealistic.
c.   reductionistic.
d.   both a and c

7. The philosophical position that views human ideas, beliefs, and values as by-products of material life, reflecting it but not shaping it, is known as
a.   dualism.
b.   interactionism.
c.   holism.
d.   materialism.

8. The attempt to explain something complex by showing that complexity is the outcome of simpler causal forces is called
   a. determinism.
   a. dualism.
   b. holism.
* c. reductionism.

9. _____ attempts to explain complex human nature in terms of a single set of determining principles.
* a. Reductionism
   b. Dualism
   c. Interactionism
   d. Holism

10. Some thinkers have tried to explain mind in terms of matter or matter in terms of mind. This is an example of
    a. Determinism.
    b. Reductionism.
    c. Interactionism.
* d. both a and b

11. Charles Darwin's innovation in his theory of natural selection was to
    a. argue for change over time.
    b. calculate that genotype and phenotype were directly related.
* c. propose a materialistic explanation for biological change.
    d. argue for the evolution of human society.

12. "You are what you learn" is a motto expressing the basic position of
    a. biological determinism.
* b. cultural determinism.
    c. dualism.
    d. none of the above

13. To argue that "you are what you are conditioned to be" is an example of
    a. biological determinism.
    b. reductionism.
    c. cultural determinism.
* d. both b and c

14. _____ attempts to explain human nature as the product of the dialectical interpenetration of object and environment.
   a. Dualism
* b Holism
   c. Reductionism
   d. none of the above

15. Karl Marx is responsible for the development of which philosophical position?
   a. biological determinism
   b. dualism
* c. historical materialism
   d. idealism

16. The claim that the collective material actions of people in society over time shape human life
   a. is called historical materialism.
   b. is a form of environmental determinism.
   c. is associated with Karl Marx.
* d. all of the above

17. The claim that human life is shaped not by biology but by physical forces external to the human species is
   a. a form of materialist reductionism.
   b. called environmental determinism.
   c. called dualism.
* d. both a and b

18. The most extreme reaction against the various forms of materialist reductionism is called
* a. cultural determinism.
   b. biological determinism.
   c. interactionism.
   d. holism.

19. The claim that the ideas, meanings, beliefs, and values that people learn as members of society determine their behavior
   a. is an idealist position.
   b. has been called cultural determinism.
   c. can be understood to imply that "you are what you are conditioned to be."
   d. all of the above

123

20. The motto "the whole is greater than the sum of its parts" describes the position of
   a.   historical materialism.
   b.   idealism.
   c.   biological determinism.
* d.   holism.

21. Clifford Geertz observes that human beings raised in isolation would be
   a.   failed apes.
   b.   fully human.
* c.   mental basket cases.
   d.   the real animal under the veneer of culture.

22. To describe parts and wholes as mutually defining, or codetermining, each other is to speak
* a.   dialectically.
   b.   interactionally.
   c.   reductionistically.
   d.   deterministically.

23. An approach to human nature, human society, and human history that views human beings and environments as open systems that modify each other is called
   a.   biological reductionism.
   b.   cultural determinism.
* c.   dialectical holism.
   d.   historical materialism.

24. Which of the following statements is true of dialectical holism?
   a.   human nature is culturally shaped.
   b.   human society is historically situated.
   c.   human beings are active agents who are required to construct their actions and choose between alternatives.
* d.   all of the above

25. A _____ perspective argues that society and individuals create each other.
* a.   dialectical
   b.   dualist
   b.   positivist
   d.   reductionist

124

26. Hoyt Alverson discovered that U.S. Peace Corps volunteers in Botswana had difficulty with their assignments in part because
   a.   people would always leave them alone.
* b.   actions that meant one thing to them meant something else to their Tswana hosts.
   c.   the Tswana were not interested in their projects.
   d.   all of the above

27. Hoyt Alverson discovered that the Tswana people he talked to in Botswana and the U.S. Peace Corps volunteers he interviewed differed with regard to
   a.   how work should be done.
* b.   the meaning of being alone.
   c.   walking through fields with crops still in them.
   d.   how anger should be expressed.

28. The opinion that one's own way of life is natural or correct and the only true way of being fully human is called
   a.   cultural relativism.
   b.   cultural determinism.
* c.   ethnocentrism.
   d.   egocentrism.

29. Understanding another culture sympathetically enough so that it appears to be a coherent and meaningful design for living is called
   a.   interactionism.
* b.   relativism.
   c.   holism.
   d.   all of the above

30. Genocide is
* a.   the attempt to exterminate an entire people.
   b.   denying that another culture has an independent identity.
   c.   the attempt to keep a group of people from living according to their own cultural patterns.
   d.   both b and c

31. Cultural relativism
   a.   requires us to abandon every value our own culture has taught us.
   b.   makes it possible for us to prove the way a people's culture makes them do things whether they like it or not.
   c.   requires us to take into account many things before we make up our minds.
   d.   frees us from having to face choices between alternatives whose "rightness" and "wrongness" is less than clear-cut.

32. Which of the following is NOT an assumption of cultural determinism regarding human nature and human society?
   a.   Cultures have clear boundaries.
   b.   Every culture offers people only one way to interpret their experience.
* c.   Every culture contains fundamental contradictions.
   d.   Human beings are passively molded by culture.

33. To argue that "their culture made them do it" is to take the position of
* a.   cultural determinism.
   b.   cultural relativism.
   c.   ethnocentrism.
   d.   environmental determinism.

34. The anthropological definition of cultural relativism requires that we make an effort to _____ the practices of other cultures
   a.   approve
   b.   excuse
   c.   judge
* d.   understand

35. When human beings exercise at least some control over their own behavior, they are said to be
* a.   agents.
   b.   cultural.
   c.   holistic.
   d.   reductionists.

Essay Questions

36. Discuss the basic principles of idealism or materialism and how each has been used in anthropology.

37. Give an actual or invented example of ethnocentrism and discuss the range of possible perspectives on the practice in question that might be held by members and outsiders of the society where it is found.

38. "Our dependence on culture is total. Without it, we cannot survive as biological organisms." Discuss.

39. The goal of cultural relativism is understanding. However, to understand does not mean to condone. How would an anthropologist, from a relativistic point of view, explain a cultural practice like genocide (for example, the Nazis' attempt to exterminate the Jews)?

40. How does dialectical holism differ from dualism and reductionism? Give examples.

41. Why is the discussion of such philosophical issues as idealism, materialism, dualism, and so on found in an anthropology text?

42. There has been an enormous amount of discussion in recent years concerning the source (and importance) of behavioral differences distinguishing men from women in our own and other cultures. Choose two of the perspectives on human nature discussed in your text and describe the way each perspective would explain particular differences between women and men.

43. What is a dialectical view of the human condition and what are its advantages?

CHAPTER 12

ETHNOGRAPHIC FIELDWORK

Outline

A MEETING OF CULTURAL TRADITIONS

THE MECHANICS OF FIELDWORK

SCIENTIFIC FIELDWORK?

The Positivist Approach
Applying Positivist Methods to Anthropology
Reflexivity

THE DIALECTIC OF FIELDWORK: INTERPRETATION AND
    TRANSITION

Interpreting Actions and Ideas
The Dialectical Process
Translating
The Dialectic between Self and Other

COMMUNICATION IN FIELDWORK: CONSTRUCTING MEANING

THE EFFECT OF FIELDWORK ON INFORMANTS

THE EFFECT OF FIELDWORK ON THE RESEARCHER

THE HUMANIZING EFFECT OF FIELDWORK

COMING UP WITH THE FACTS OF ANTHROPOLOGY

ANTHROPOLOGICAL KNOWLEDGE AS OPEN-ENDED

Key Terms

fieldwork	objective knowledge	interpretation
culture shock	informants	translation
participant-observation	intersubjective meanings	facts
positivism	reflexivity	

Arguing Anthropology

1. What is the value of culture shock?

2. If the facts of cultural anthropology are "constructed," does cultural
    anthropology become just one person's opinion?

Multiple Choice Questions

1. Why did the Quichua-speakers of Otavalo, Ecuador invite the anthropologist Lawrence Carpenter to drink chicha with them?
   - a. They had accepted him as a part of the group.
   - b. They wanted him to experience their traditional feasting.
   - * c. They wanted to test him.
   - d. They felt that he would be able to learn more of their language by drinking with them.

2. The ethnographic research method that relies primarily on face-to-face contact with people as they go about their daily lives is called
   - a. controlled comparison.
   - b. interviewing.
   - c. scientific observation.
   - * d. participant observation.

3. An extended period of research during which an anthropologist gathers firsthand data about life in a particular society is called
   - * a. fieldwork.
   - b. graduate school.
   - c. scientific observation.
   - d. controlled comparison.

4. Which of the following research methods is NOT used by cultural anthropologists?
   - a. archival and library research
   - b. psychological testing
   - c. questionnaire administration
   - * d. All of the above are used.

5. Cultural anthropological fieldwork is
   - a. not always done in a non-Western society.
   - b. responsible for the majority of anthropological knowledge.
   - c. a collaborative effort on the part of both anthropologist and informant.
   - * d. all of the above.

6. The jolt that often accompanies an encounter with cultural practices that are unexpected and strange is called
   - a. participant-observation.
   - b. fieldwork.
   - c. dialogue.
   - * d. culture shock.

129

7. The text suggests that fieldwork and culture shock are related in which of the following ways?
    a.   Fieldwork permits culture shock to be avoided.
* b.   Fieldwork institutionalizes culture shock.
    c.   Culture shock makes cross-cultural learning very difficult.
    d.   Culture shock distorts the data gathered through fieldwork.

8. Which of the following phrases describes the kinds of people who tend to become an anthropologist's key informants?
    a.   They are able to give external form to their own experiences by presenting them to meet the anthropologist's questions.
    b.   They tend to be rather marginal in their own societies.
    c.   They have the ability to explain even the most obvious things to a foreigner in a variety of ways.
* d.   all of the above

9. How do anthropologists obtain funding for their research?
    a.   They pay for it themselves.
    b.   They get research grants from private agencies.
* c.   They get research grants from governmental agencies.
    d.   all of the above

10. Which of the following is a principle of positivist science?
    a.   Reality can be known through the five senses.
    b.   A single scientific method can be used to investigate any domain of reality.
    c.   Facts and values are separate from one another.
* d.   All of the above are true.

11. Positivists accept
    a.   that facts relate to the nature of physical reality—what is.
    b.   that all scientific knowledge will ultimately be unified.
    c.   a form of materialist reductionism.
* d.   all of the above

12. The belief that facts and values have nothing to do with each other is a principle of
* a.   positivism.
    b.   anthropology.
    c.   intersubjectivity.
    d.   none of the above

130

13. The production of objective knowledge about reality which is absolute and true for all times and places is a goal of
   a.   anthropology.
   b.   intersubjectivity.
* c.   positivism.
   d.   fieldwork.

14. Anthropological knowledge is
   a.   subjective.
   b.   objective.
* c.   intersubjective.
   d.   all of the above

15. The debate over Margaret Mead's interpretation of adolescence in Samoa was based on
   a.   a misconception of the nature of field research.
* b.   a difference in assumptions.
   c.   Mead's error-filled fieldwork.
   d.   changing standards of field research.

16. Which of the following pairs of anthropologists did fieldwork in the Trobriand Islands?
   a.   Freeman and Mead
   b.   Kumar and Valentine
   c.   Rabinow and Briggs
* d.   Weiner and Malinowski

17. According to the text, all anthropological knowledge is a product of the dialectic between observation and
   a.   ethnocentrism.
* b.   reflection.
   c.   science.
   d.   subjectivity.

18. The subject matter of the social sciences differs in one major respect from the subject matter of the physical sciences in that
* a.   it involves human beings who belong to the same species (and possibly the same society) as the scientists themselves.
   b.   social scientific facts are separate from social values.
   c.   physical scientists can capture objective samples of reality, whereas social scientists cannot.
   d.   the presence of an observer makes no difference in the physical sciences but makes a great deal of difference in the social sciences.

19. According to the text, what keeps cultural anthropology from being one person's subjective impressions of other people?
* a.   the fact that fieldwork is a dialogue
   b.   the fact that anthropology is a scientific discipline
   c.   the fact that anthropologists are trained to avoid ethnocentrism
   d.   Nothing; that's what cultural anthropology is.

20. The term anthropologists conventionally use to refer to the people in the culture from whom they gather data is
   a.   associates.
   b.   informers.
* c.   informants.
   d.   intersubjects.

21. Recognizing the humanity of one's informants has nothing to do with trying to come up with a subjective, imaginative impression of what it must be like to live their lives. This is because
   a.   informants do not have inner lives.
* b.   such imaginative effort is solitary, whereas fieldwork is a dialogue.
   c.   objectivity requires anthropologists to avoid identifying with their informants.
   d.   getting your informants' opinions about things contaminates the data.

22. Reflexivity is
   a.   an automatic response.
   b.   a key principle of positivist science.
   c.   the outcome of objective observation and dispassionate analysis.
* d.   thinking about thinking.

23. In her published ethnography, anthropologist Bettylou Valentine states her own conclusions, but she also allows her informants a voice, permitting them, in a final chapter, to state where and why they disagree with her. Such an ethnography is
   a.   an example of incomplete analysis.
   b.   an example of reflexive analysis.
   c.   a vivid experience of the open-endedness of the dialogue between anthropologist and informant.
* d.   both b and c

24. Hermeneutics means
* a.   interpretation.
   b.   objectivity.
   c.   translation.
   d.   fieldwork.

25. According to Paul Rabinow, the comprehension of the cultural self by the detour of the comprehension of the cultural other
* a.   is the central problem of interpretation in the fieldwork context.
  b.   leads anthropologist and informant to enter into the dialectic of fieldwork.
  c.   can produce cross-cultural facts.
  d.   all of the above

26. Even if an anthropologist and informants are from very different cultures with different languages, what do they share?
  a.   a common humanity
* b.   the fieldwork situation
  c.   an understanding of each others' motives
  d.   nothing

27. When early anthropologists tried to test their hypotheses in a series of different cultural settings in an attempt to approximate the laboratory conditions of a positivist scientist, they were employing
  a.   statistical sampling.
  b.   the dialectic of fieldwork.
* c.   the method of controlled comparison.
  d.   none of the above

28. The dialectic of fieldwork refers to
  a.   the personal and financial connection between the anthropologist and the informants.
  b.   the anthropologist's knowledge that he or she will return home while the informants must stay.
* c.   the mutual construction of cross-cultural knowledge about the informant's culture by anthropologist and informant together.
  d.   the gradual discovery of the truth about a society through the anthropologist's careful research.

29. The dialectic of fieldwork leads to the construction and growth of cultural anthropological knowledge because
  a.   good anthropologists are always fluent in the language of their informants.
* b.   both anthropologist and informant are active agents.
  c.   key informants are usually bicultural.
  d.   the informant is always right.

30. Some anthropologists claim that anthropological fieldwork is a process of mutual
    a.   awareness.
    b.   debate.
    c.   interaction.
* d.   translation.

31. The questions that anthropologists ask in the field are determined by
    a.   their informants.
    b.   the field situation itself.
* c.   the discipline of anthropology.
    d.   their perceptions of the needs of the moment.

32. The difficulties faced by Nita Kumar in her fieldwork in Banaras were in part a result of
    a.   being a woman.
* b.   being Indian.
    c.   being a foreigner.
    d.   knowing too much about the weavers with whom she wished to work.

33. Which of the following was NOT a way in which Nita Kumar was removed from the people of Banaras with whom she worked?
* a.   age
    b.   education and upbringing
    c.   language
    d.   region

34. An unwritten rule of thumb for fieldworkers has long been summed up in the motto:
* a.   The informant is always right.
    b.   Never become romantically involved.
    c.   Never on Sunday.
    d.   Questions must be understood by the informants.

35. When Paul Rabinow found that Ibrahim had made up a story about relatives in another city in order to try to get Rabinow to pay for the trip, he discovered
    a.   that he could trust no one in Morocco.
* b.   the shock of otherness.
    c.   the correctness of his informants.
    d.   the surprise of pseudofriendship.

36. What was the consequence of Rabinow's anger towards Ali that prompted him to let Ali out of the car?
   a. Ali refused to have any more to do with him.
   b. It took Rabinow months of work to reestablish good relations with other Moroccans.
 * c. His relationship with Ali improved.
   d. Although he and Ali made up, their relationship had cooled.

37. The differences between the field experiences of Paul Rabinow and those of Jean Briggs illustrate
   a. the significance of ruptures of communication in fieldwork.
   b. the difficulty of knowing what appropriate behavior in a particular society might be.
   c. the importance of local knowledge in field research.
 * d. all of the above

38. Field data are the product of long discussions between researcher and informant, of patient and painstaking collaborative attempts between them to sort things out, piece things together, to make sense of a shared world. In a word, they are
   a. objective.
   b. subjective.
   c. non-objective.
 * d. intersubjective.

39. When do the facts of anthropology speak for themselves?
   a. when anthropologist and informant talk together
   b. when a well trained anthropologist has spent several months in the field
   c. when they are presented in an anthropological monograph
 * d. never

40. Why were the Utku scandalized when Jean Briggs openly expressed her anger to the white fisherman who damaged their canoes?
   a. because the fisherman had paid for the damage
 * b. because she was an adopted daughter who had spoken unbidden and in anger
   c. because an anthropologist shouldn't attempt to resolve local conflicts
   d. because she directed anger toward her own people

41. Learning about another culture is often greatest
a.   once the anthropologist has been accepted as a member of the group.
b.   once the anthropologist learns to live by the motto "the informant is always right."
*   c.   following a rupture of communication between anthropologist and informant.
d.   once the anthropologist has learned to avoid culture shock

Essay Questions

42. Fieldwork institutionalizes shock. How does this fact affect the way anthropological knowledge is constructed?

43. Participant-observation is the classic method of anthropological research. Many anthropologists would argue that no proper understanding of another culture can be attained without it. What is so valuable about participant-observation? What would be missed if anthropologists did not engage in it during fieldwork?

44. What kinds of preparations do anthropologists make before going into the field, and why?

45. Give an example of a reflexive experience you may have had and explain how this affected your views of yourself and your own culture.

46. Facts do not speak for themselves but must be interpreted. Discuss.

47. What are the advantages and disadvantages of the positivist approach to anthropological research?

48. Discuss the effects of fieldwork on the informant and on the researcher.

49. Rabinow writes, "There is no primitive, there are only other men leading other lives." What does he mean? What are the implications of such a view for the way anthropologists carry out their research?

CHAPTER 13

HISTORY, ANTHROPOLOGY, AND
THE EXPLANATION OF CULTURAL DIVERSITY

Outline

HUMAN IMAGINATION AND THE MATERIAL WORLD

CROSS-CULTURAL CONTACTS BETWEEN THE WEST AND THE REST
    OF THE WORLD

THE EFFECTS OF WESTERN EXPANSION

Expansion in Africa and the Americas
The Fur Trade in North America
The Slave and Commodities Trades

TOWARD CLASSIFYING FORMS OF HUMAN SOCIETY

Evolutionary Typologies: The Nineteenth Century
Social Structural Typologies: The British Emphasis
Doing Without Typologies: Culture Area Studies in America
Postwar Realities
Studying Forms of Human Society Today

Key Terms

typology	band	structural-functional
unilineal cultural	tribe	theory
evolutionism	chiefdom	culture traits
social structure	state	culture area

Arguing Anthropology

1. How have the contacts between the West and the rest of the world affected the development of anthropology?

2. How do the classifications of societies available at any given moment shape people's political and economic decisions?

Multiple Choice Questions

1. The scientific value of typology depends on
  a.   the truthfulness of the categories.
* b.   the usefulness of the categories.
  c.   the size of the categories.
  d.   the cultural appropriateness of the categories.

2. The Five-Element Theory in China
    a.   is confirmed by Western science.
    b.   is actually the same as the Greek theory of the elements.
* c.   was as helpful to early scientific thought in China as the Greek theory
         of the elements was to the development of Western science.
    d.   all of the above

3. According to the authors, cultural traditions take shape as a result of the
   dialectic between
    a.   society and economy.
* b.   the possibilities we can imagine and the likelihood of realizing those
         possibilities in the material world.
    c.   religion and science.
    d.   none of the above

4. Classifications of human societies help us to
    a.   see reality in an undistorted way.
    b.   perceive the sharp boundaries that separate societies from one another.
* c.   see some of the ways societies are similar and different, while obscuring
         others.
    d.   both a and b

5. Western European contact with the rest of the world was
    a.   neutral.
* b.   eventually aimed at conquest.
    c.   egalitarian.
    d.   concerned with trade and commerce.

6. In the societies they have visited, anthropologists have usually been
   preceded for many years by explorers, colonial administrators, and
   missionaries. This illustrates the maxim
    a.   the informant is always right.
    b.   people outside the Western world are people without history.
    c.   might makes right.
* d.   there is no such thing as pre-contact ethnography.

7. When Europeans arrived in Africa,
    a.   European conquest was immediate and disastrous.
    b.   European diseases effectively wiped out large portions of local
         populations who lacked immunity.
* c.   they found themselves confined to the coast for more than 400 hundred
         years.
    d.   both a and b

8. In the wake of European exploration, conquest, colonization, and decolonization, which of the following statements about the fate of all non-Western peoples is false?
   a. European contact affected these societies in a radical way.
   b. Remnants of precontact societies survive today.
   c. An impressive variety of forms of human society remain in spite of the Western onslaught.
 * d. Life in the non-Western world today remains timeless and unchanged.

9. Which of the following European countries was the first to explore and expand beyond the borders of Europe?
   a. England
   b. France
 * c. Portugal
   d. Spain

10. When Europeans first established commercial relationships in Africa,
   a. within 10 years, they had conquered deeply into the continent.
   b. the Africans welcomed them as liberators from the cruel rulers of the coastal empires.
 * c. they were not allowed to penetrate very far inland for more than 400 years.
   d. the coastal African peoples controlled the trade for more than 100 years.

11. With regard to disease and European contact with Africa and the Americas,
 * a. in the Americas, the indigenous people were devastated by disease, whereas in Africa, the Europeans were affected.
   b. in the Americas, the Europeans were devastated by disease, whereas in Africa, the indigenous people were affected.
   c. in both Africa and the Americas, disease was not as significant as commercial relations.
   d. in the Americas, disease was only one factor in the European conquest, whereas in Africa it was the major factor.

12. Which of the following was an effect of the fur trade on the indigenous people of North America?
   a. They were able to ignore it for long periods of time.
 * b. It caused serious problems for those groups that were dedicated to it when the fur-bearing animals were gone.
   c. It led to the development of close ties between indigenous peoples and the major nations of Europe, which had an important influence on the help the Europeans were able to provide when the fur-bearing animals were gone.
   d. Both b and c are true.

13. The Midewiwin was
   a.   a traditional set of rituals that was used by the Ojibway and their neighbors to prepare for fur-trapping.
* b.   a set of rituals that was developed by the Ojibway and their neighbors as a response to contact with European fur traders.
   c.   a seventeenth-century ritual attempt by the Ojibway and their neighbors to rid North America of Europeans.
   d.   a set of rituals that incorporated the European fur traders into traditional Ojibway religion.

14. One effect of the slave trade was to
* a.   draw Africa, Europe, and America increasingly tightly together.
   b.   increase the birth rate in Africa and Europe.
   c.   reduce the number of Native American peoples.
   d.   all of the above

15. One way that anthropologists make sense of the variety of forms of human society across space and over time is through
   a.   seeking the universals of the human experience.
   b.   analyzing the characteristics of each individual society.
* c.   sorting societies into distinct categories.
   d.   all of the above

16. When Europeans in the Age of Discovery were first getting to know other societies, they were most struck by
   a.   the sophistication of nonWestern peoples.
* b.   all the social forms these societies seemed to lack.
   c.   the universality of organized religion.
   d.   the universal use of money as a medium of exchange.

17. The theory that proposed a series of stages through which all societies had passed or must pass in order to reach civilization is called
   a.   culture area theory.
   b.   diffusionism.
   c.   structural-functional theory.
* d.   unilineal cultural evolutionism.

18. A proponent of unilineal evolutionary theory who had widespread influence is
   a.   E. E. Evans-Pritchard.
   b.   Claude Lévi-Strauss.
* c.   Lewis Henry Morgan.
   d.   Benjamin Lee Whorf.

19. In Morgan's evolutionary system, all groups that never attained the art of pottery were classed as
* a.   savages.
  b.   barbarians.
  c.   civilized.
  d.   none of the above

20. Which of the following was NOT a stage in the unilineal cultural evolutionists' model?
  a.   barbarism
  b.   civilization
  c.   savagery
* d.   tribal

21. According to Morgan, those groups possessing the art of pottery but who have never attained a phonetic alphabet and the art of writing were classified as
  a.   savages.
* b.   barbarians.
  c.   civilized.
  d.   none of the above

22. Colonial officials were often distrustful of anthropologists' motives because
  a.   the sympathies of anthropologists often lay with the colonized people among whom they worked.
  b.   it was all too likely that the results of anthropological research might make colonial programs look self-serving and exploitative.
  c.   many anthropologists who carried out fieldwork under colonial conditions were not supporters of colonialism.
* d.   all of the above

23. In Africa, British officials occupied the top of the colonial hierarchy and employed traditional rulers (elders, chiefs, etc.) as their intermediaries with the common people. This is referred to as
  a.   direct exchange.
  b.   direct rule.
  c.   indirect exchange.
* d.   indirect rule.

24. British anthropologists call themselves social anthropologists because of their focus on
   a.　　social evolution.
* b.　　social structure.
   c.　　socialism.
   d.　　socialization processes.

25. The creation of a structural-functional typology of African political systems was the outcome of work by
* a.　　Fortes and Evans-Pritchard.
   b.　　Lévi-Strauss and Morgan.
   c.　　Lewellyn and Radcliffe-Brown.
   d.　　Malinowski and Boas.

26. Those anthropologists who are most likely to rely on typologies of human societies today are those who study
   a.　　art and religion.
   b.　　linguistics and literature.
* c.　　politics and economics.
   d.　　all of the above rely on typologies.

27. Which of the following persons believed that culture change was due more to borrowing from neighboring societies than to independent invention?
* a.　　Boas
   b.　　Evans-Pritchard
   c.　　Malinowski
   d.　　Radcliffe-Brown

28. The enduring aspects of a society's social forms, including its political and kinship systems, are called
   a.　　culture areas.
   b.　　preindustrial political systems.
* c.　　social structures.
   d.　　taxonomies.

29. Which of the following statements accurately characterizes the structural-functional approach to social typology?
   a.　　Questions of evolution and social change are uppermost.
   b.　　It is based on a decisive refutation of unilineal evolutionism.
   c.　　The terms savagery, barbarism, and civilization are no longer used by those who favor this approach.
* d.　　The emphasis is on how traditional structures of societies endure over time.

30. The major distinction in the contemporary social structural classification of forms of human societies discussed in the text is between _____ and _____ societies.
   * a. centralized; egalitarian
   b. centralized; band
   c. egalitarian; band
   d. egalitarian; tribal

31. A small, egalitarian social grouping whose members neither farm nor herd, but depend on wild food resources is called a
   * a. band.
   b. tribe.
   c. chiefdom.
   d. state.

32. An egalitarian society whose members raise domesticated plants or animals for food is known as a
   a. band.
   * b. tribe.
   c. chiefdom.
   d. state.

33. A rank society with minimal social stratification is called a
   a. band.
   b. tribe.
   * c. chiefdom.
   d. state.

34. A hierarchical, stratified society in which some groups monopolize wealth, power, and prestige is called a
   a. band.
   b. tribe.
   c. chiefdom.
   * d. state.

35. Which of the following approaches to the diversity of human social forms does not rely on typologies of individual societies?
   a. unilineal cultural evolutionism
   b. structural-functionalism
   * c. culture area studies
   d. political anthropology

36. A single element or part of a cultural tradition, such as a dance or a way of making pots, is called a
   a.   typology.
 * b.   culture trait.
   c.   culture area.
   d.   social structure.

37. The term culture area refers to
   a.   a geographical region in which a particular stage of cultural evolution has been reached.
   b.   a geographical region in which all societies can be classified as representatives of the same structural-functional type.
 * c.   a geographical region marking the limits of the diffusion of a particular cultural trait or set of traits.
   d.   a geographical region within whose boundaries all people share the same culture.

38. The voices of non-Western anthropologists have been most influential during which period?
   a.   the Age of Discovery
   b.   the period of Western colonization of the nonWestern world
 * c.   following the breakup of Western colonial empires
   d.   prior to Western contact

39. Many anthropologists would insist that an important watershed in social organization is marked by a shift from
   a.   foraging for wild foods to depending on domesticated plants and animals for food.
   b.   egalitarian societies to stratified societies.
   c.   organization in terms of kinship to organization in terms of social class.
 * d.   all of the above

40. Which of the following factors sets the native peoples of the northwest coast of North America apart from other foragers?
   a.   They possess no domesticated animals.
 * b.   They live in large, settled villages.
   c.   Their social organization is highly egalitarian.
   d.   They eat fish.

Essay Questions

41. Discuss the effect of contact with Europe on indigenous peoples in Africa and in the Americas.

42. Why do anthropologists attempt to classify different forms of human society? What are the advantages and limitations of typologies?

43. Discuss British social anthropology, paying particular attention to the intellectual and political context within which it developed.

44. What historical circumstances influenced the development of unilineal cultural evolutionism? What are the strengths and weaknesses of unilineal typologies such as the one proposed by Morgan? Discuss.

45. Both British and American anthropologists eventually came to reject unilineal cultural evolutionism. But each group replaced it with a different approach for dealing with the variety of human social forms. What were these approaches? How did they differ, both from each other and from unilineal cultural evolutionism?

CHAPTER 14

LANGUAGE

Outline

LANGUAGE AND CULTURE

Anthropological Interest in Language
Talking about Experience

DESIGN FEATURES OF HUMAN LANGUAGE

Opening Closed Call Systems

LANGUAGE AND COGNITION

THE SAPIR-WHORF HYPOTHESIS

COMPONENTS OF LANGUAGE

Phonology: Sounds
Morphology: Word Structure
Syntax: Sentence Structure
Semantics: Meaning
Pragmatics: Language in Contexts of Use

LINGUISTICS INEQUALITY

Speech in the Inner City
Speech of Women and Men

THE DIALECTIC BETWEEN LANGUAGE AND CULTURE

Schemas
Prototypes
Metaphors

PIDGIN LANGUAGES: NEGOTIATING MEANING

LANGUAGE AND TRUTH

Key Terms

language
linguistics
design features
cognition
linguistic competence
communicative
  competence

Sapir-Whorf hypothesis
phonology
morphology
syntax
semantics
pragmatics

schemas
prototypes
metaphors
pidgin

Arguing Anthropology

1. Does language determine thought?

2. Do you think that men and women in the United States "speak the same language?"

Multiple Choice Questions

1. Language, like culture, is
a. learned.
b. coded in symbols.
c. shared.
d. all of the above

2. Which of the following is NOT a reason for anthropological interest in language?
a. Fieldworkers need to communicate with their informants.
b. Language can be lifted out of its cultural context and analyzed on its own.
c. Language is the single most important element of any culture; to understand language is to understand another culture fully.
d. Language is the way people encode their experience and structure their understanding of the world.

3. The transfer of information from one person to another is
a. communication.
b. language.
c. Language.
d. speech.

4. What is the difference between speech and language?
a. Speech is spoken language.
b. Language is a kind of speech.
c. Language and speech are both forms of language.
d. There is no difference between the two.

5. "Primitive" languages
a. have a limited vocabulary.
b. lack elaborate grammatical structure.
c. make use of a reduced set of sounds.
d. do not exist.

6. Which of the following statements is true of speech communities?
   a.   Members of a speech community have no difficulties in understanding one another.
* b.   Members of a speech community do not all possess identical knowledge about the language they share.
   c.   Members of a speech community use the varied resources of their common language in the same way.
   d.   Both a and b are true.

7. Which of the following statements about a speech community is true?
   a.   All members possess identical knowledge about the language.
   b.   There is no tension involved in verbal communication since all members use the same set of linguistic forms.
   c.   Consensus does not need to be negotiated.
* d.   none of the above

8. Differences across languages
   a.   are absolute.
   b.   are superficial.
* c.   are most often differences in context or frequency of use.
   d.   are based in differences in physiology.

9. The design features of language called "openness" refers to the
   a.   possibility of speaking without fear of a censor.
   b.   capacity of putting our true feelings into words.
* c.   ability to create new linguistic messages freely and easily.
   d.   connection between sound and brain.

10. The number of calls in the vocal communication systems of apes are few, and any particular call is produced only when the animal finds itself in a particular situation. Thus, ape vocal communication systems lack the linguistic design feature of
* a.   openness.
   b.   rapid fading.
   c.   interchangeability.
   d.   specialization.

11. Hockett and Ascher suggest that a major switch in human evolution occurred when
* a.   the closed call systems of our ape ancestors opened up.
   b.   writing became important in human affairs.
   c.   our ape ancestors became able to communicate orally.
   d.   the earliest proto-humans became the first creatures to communicate about things that were not present.

148

12. Nonhuman primates cannot communicate vocally about absent or nonexistent objects or past or future events. Thus, their call systems lack the linguistic design feature of
    a.   complete feedback.
*   b.   displacement.
    c.   discreteness.
    d.   semanticity.

13. "Displacement" in language refers to the
    a.   tip-of-the-tongue phenomena.
*   b.   ability to refer to things remote in time or place.
    c.   use of foreign terms in one's native language.
    d.   ability to talk and breathe at the same time.

14. In ape call systems, the link between the sound of a call and its meaning appears to be fixed and under considerable direct biological control. Thus, ape call systems lack the linguistic design feature of
    a.   displacement.
    b.   duality of patterning.
*   c.   arbitrariness.
    d.   discreteness.

15. There is nothing inherent in the nature of a large quadruped well-suited for long distance running that requires us to call this creature a "horse." This illustrates the linguistic design feature of
    a.   specialization.
    b.   definition.
    c.   semanticity.
*   d.   arbitrariness.

16. Human languages are patterned at different levels, and the patterns that characterize one level cannot be reduced to the pattern of any other level. Hockett recognized this phenomenon in which of his linguistic design features?
*   a.   duality of patterning
    b.   reflexiveness
    c.   specialization
    d.   displacement

17. The association of linguistic signals with aspects of the social, cultural, and physical world of a speech community is called
   a.   displacement.
   b.   duality of patterning.
   c.   openness.
* d.   semanticity.

18. Linguistic messages can be false, and they can be meaningless in the logician's sense. This highlights the linguistic design feature of
   a.   interchangeability.
* b.   prevarication.
   c.   duality of patterning.
   d.   reflexiveness.

19. Which design feature of language accounts for the ability to lie and to formulate hypotheses?
* a.   prevarication
   b.   semanticity
   c.   duality of patterning
   d.   discreteness

20. The mental processes by which human beings gain knowledge is called
   a.   arbitrariness.
* b.   cognition.
   c.   language.
   d.   testing.

21. The ability of native speakers of a language to distinguish correctly between grammatical and ungrammatical sentences is called
   a.   duality of patterning.
   b.   interchangeability.
   c.   communicative competence.
* d.   linguistic competence.

22. The ability of native speakers of a language to use words in ways that are socially and culturally appropriate is called
   a.   specialization.
   b.   discreteness.
* c.   communicative competence.
   d.   linguistic competence.

23. In Java it is impossible to
   a.   give a one-word answer.
   b.   refer directly to your mother-in-law.
* c.   say anything without communicating your relative social position.
   d.   none of the above

24. The concept of cognitive openness refers to
* a.   the ability to understand the same thing from different points of view.
   b.   the way thought determines language.
   c.   the way language determines thought.
   d.   the ability to form opinions that accord with cultural values.

25. Edward Sapir and Benjamin Lee Whorf believed that
   a.   language determines thought.
   b.   thought determines language.
* c.   language has the power to shape the way people see the world.
   d.   None of the above are true.

26. Linguistic determinism holds that
* a.   the grammars of our native languages determine how we think about
            the world.
   b.   how we speak determines our likelihood for success.
   c.   language is the basis for culture.
   d.   Both a and c are true.

27. Phonology, morphology, syntax, semantics, and pragmatics are components
    of
   a.   sentence structure.
   b.   the sound system of language.
   c.   meaning.
* d.   language.

28. The study of sounds is called
* a.   phonology.
   b.   morphology.
   c.   syntax.
   d.   semantics.

29. Which component of language is concerned with the way in which words are put together?
    a.   phonology.
* b.   morphology.
    c.   syntax.
    d.   semantics.

30. American English recognizes 38 significant sounds. These are called
    a.   consonants.
* b.   phonemes.
    c.   phonology.
    d.   the auditory system.

31. The minimal units of meaning in language are referred to as
    a.   root words.
* b.   morphemes.
    c.   affixes.
    d.   all of the above

32. The concept of the morpheme was helpful to linguists because
    a.   it allowed them to break down phonemes into their distinctive features.
* b.   it allowed them to refer both to the words in a language like English and to the meaning-bearing parts of utterances in languages like Shawnee.
    c.   it allowed them to construct operational definitions for the first time.
    d.   it allowed them to distinguish denotation from connotation.

33. How many morphemes are in the sentence, "John and Sally walked home"?
    a.   4
    b.   5
* c.   6
    d.   7

34. The way in which patterns of words are put together into sentences is called
    a.   phonology.
    b.   morphology.
* c.   syntax.
    d.   semantics.

35. According to Chomsky, a sentence like "The girl fixed the clock" can be changed into "The clock was fixed by the girl" by means of
   a.   a deep structure.
   b.   a surface structure.
   c.   an operational definition.
* d.   a transformational rule.

36. Surface structure and deep structure in syntax were described by
* a.   Chomsky.
   b.   Hymes.
   c.   Bloomfield.
   d.   none of the above

37. Which of the following sentences shows structural ambiguity?
   a.   You have failed this exam.
* b.   Flying planes can be dangerous.
   c.   Come over sometime tomorrow.
   d.   The dog is on the rug.

38. Semantics is
   a.   the study of meaning.
   b.   an area of linguistics which was late to develop.
   c.   an area which studies language use in context.
* d.   both a and b

39. Referring to a police officer as a pig is an example of
   a.   radical politics.
* b.   connotation.
   c.   syntax.
   d.   denotation.

40. The dictionary definition of a word is an example of
   a.   deep structure.
   b.   surface structure.
   c.   connotation.
   d.   denotation.

41. The study of the way speakers of a language actually use the language to communicate with one another is called
   a.   pragmatics.
   b.   syntax.
   c.   reflexivity.
   d.   phonetics.

42. A stretch of speech longer than a sentence, united by a common theme, is called
   a.   deep structure.
   b.   surface structure.
* c.   discourse.
   d.   pragmatics.

43. Linguistic context refers to the other _____ that surround the expression whose meaning is being determined.
   a.   words
   b.   expressions
   c.   sentences
* d.   all of the above

44. In the course of conversation, different speakers may represent elements of the same nonlinguistic context differently. That is, each speaker
   a.   takes up a different referential perspective with regard to the context.
   b.   takes up a different ideological perspective with regard to the context.
   c.   is incapable of escaping the categories of his language to learn to see the world in a different way.
* d.   both a and b

45. According to William Labov's work in the 1960s, African-American children living in urban areas did not perform well linguistically in the classroom because they
   a.   were linguistically deprived.
* b.   felt threatened in the classroom context.
   c.   had nothing to say.
   d.   all of the above

46. With regard to the speech of women and men, Deborah Tannen argues that
   a.   men and women can never understand each other.
* b.   men and women use language for different reasons.
   c.   men use language to unite themselves with other men.
   d.   men and women can communicate only when they have agreed on the basis for the conversation.

47. A patterned, repetitive experience that appears to hang together as a whole, exhibiting the same properties in the same configuration whenever it recurs is called a

* a.   schema.
  b.   prototype.
  c.   metaphor.
  d.   surface structure.

48. Examples of typical instances, elements, relations, or experiences within a particular culturally relevant domain are called

* a.   prototypes.
  b.   schemas.
  c.   metaphors.
  d.   denotations.

49. A form of thought and language that asserts a meaningful link between two expressions from different semantic domains is called

  a.   a schema.
* b.   metaphor.
  c.   a prototype.
  d.   literal language.

50. Which of the following statements about pidgin languages are true?

  a.   Pidgins are languages with no native speakers.
  b.   A pidgin language cannot be reduced to either of the languages that gave birth to it.
  c.   The study of pidgin languages is the study of the radical negotiation of new meaning.
* d.   All of the above are true.

Essay Questions

51. Language has been a central focus of anthropological interest for at least three reasons. List these reasons and discuss why they are important.

52. Adopted children commonly refer to their new parents as "mother" and "father." What does this usage suggest about the relationship between literal and metaphorical language?

53. "There is no moment at which a particular pidgin suddenly comes into existence, but rather a process of variety-creation called pidginization, by which pidgin is gradually built up out of nothing." What does this suggest about the nature of human language? Discuss in relation to the design features of language suggested by Hockett.

54. Six design features of language were singled out in the text for particular attention. Which features were they, and why are they so important?

55. Discuss the three kinds of context which influence the meaning of our speech.

56. What is a referential perspective? Discuss how referential perspectives are related to language use in particular contexts.

57. What are the five components of language? Why do linguists find it necessary to analyze language in terms of different components? What does this suggest about the nature of human language?

58. Why is the study of metaphor important to understanding the nature of language?

CHAPTER 15

COGNITION

Outline

COGNITION AS AN OPEN SYSTEM

Cognitive Capacities and Intelligence

PERCEPTION

Illusion
Cognitive Style

CONCEPTION

Reasoning and Reasoning Process
Culture and Logic

EMOTION

Emotion in an Eastern African Culture
Emotion in Oceania

THE PROCESS OF SOCIALIZATION AND ENCULTURATION

Freud and Emotional Development
Piaget and Rational Development
Mead and Vygotsky: Social dnd Sociohistorical Development

IS COGNITIVE DEVELOPMENT THE SAME FOR EVERYONE?

COGNITION AND CONTEXT

Key Terms

cognitive capacities
elementary cognitive
  processes
functional cognitive
  systems
perception

cognitive style
global style
articulated style
cognition
rational thinking
syllogistic reasoning

reasoning styles
logic
emotion
socialization
enculturation
self

Arguing Anthropology

1. Can cross-cultural relationships (ranging from ethnographic fieldwork to friendship to love and long-term intimate relationships) survive the cultural differences in perception, conception, and especially emotion?

2. If the zone of proximal development is so important in understanding learning, why do many Western people consider it to be a form of cheating?

Multiple Choice Questions

1. Cognition is often thought to have which three aspects?
   a.   illusion, perception, conception
   b.   perception, illusion, emotion
   c.   perception, paradox, conception
 * d.   perception, intellect, emotion

2. Although five senses are involved in human perception, human beings seem to rely most on
   a.   touch.
   b.   smell.
 * c.   sight.
   d.   intuition.

3. Elementary cognitive processes include the ability to
   a.   make abstractions.
   b.   categorize.
   c.   reason inferentially.
 * d.   all of the above

4. The ability to make abstractions, to categorize, to reason inferentially, and so forth is called
 * a.   elementary cognitive processes.
   b.   functional cognitive processes.
   c.   intelligence.
   d.   perception.

5. Culturally linked sets of elementary cognitive processes that guide perception, conception, reason, and emotion are called
   a.   intelligence.
 * b.   functional cognitive systems.
   c.   cognitive capacities.
   d.   none of the above

6. Distortion, paradox, ambiguity, and fiction are four types of
* a.   illusion.
  b.   conception.
  c.   perception.
  d.   syllogism.

7. Perceptions are shaped by our
  a.   genetics.
* b.   habitual experience.
  c.   nervous systems.
  d.   none of the above

8. Processes by which people organize and experience information that is primarily of sensory origin can be called
  a.   intellect.
  b.   cognition.
  c.   emotion.
* d.   perception.

9. Vygotsky's work is of particular interest to cognitive anthropologists because
  a.   he wanted to create a psychology that was compatible with a marxian analysis of society.
* b.   his ideas about cognitive development pay attention to the social, cultural, and historical context in which individual action is embedded.
  c.   he believes that a child's knowledge of the world must come through his or her own self-generated operations.
  d.   he believes that children are fully able to make sense of the world without the guidance of others.

10. When we compare the Western interpretation of the Ponzo illusion with the African interpretation of the man, elephant, and antelope drawing, what important discovery emerges?
  a.   People who are not familiar with railroad tracks cannot read two-dimensional drawings of railroad tracks.
  b.   Both sets of drawings are ambiguous.
  c.   Both sets of drawings are potentially open to distortion.
* d.   Both b and c are true.

11. When what you see appears larger or smaller, longer or shorter, than it really is, you are experiencing the visual illusion known as
* a.   distortion.
  b.   ambiguity.
  c.   paradox.
  d.   fiction.

12. The illusion that occurs when the set of visual signals is constant but the perceiver's awareness of it flips from one image to another is called
  a.   distortion.
* b.   ambiguity.
  c.   paradox.
  d.   fiction.

13. The perceptual illusion you experience when a visual image appears to be visually contradictory is called
  a.   distortion.
  b.   ambiguity.
* c.   paradox.
  d.   fiction.

14. The perceptual illusion in which the viewer sees things that are not there is called
  a.   distortion.
  b.   ambiguity.
  c.   paradox.
* d.   fiction.

15. People with a global cognitive style are said to
  a.   view the world holistically.
  b.   first see only a bundle of relationships and only later the bits and pieces that are related.
  c.   be field dependent.
* d.   all of the above

16. People with an articulated cognitive style are said to
* a.   break up the world into smaller and smaller pieces, which can then be organized.
  b.   have problems perceiving a boundary between their own bodies and the outside world.
  c.   are unable to consider whatever they happen to be paying attention to apart from its context.
  d.   all of the above

17. field dependent:field independent::
* a.   global:articulated
  b.   distant:near
  c.   trees:forest
  d.   both a and c

18. Jean Lave's research on supermarket shoppers showed that
  a.   Americans consistently used an articulated style when making best buy decisions.
  b.   Americans consistently used a global style when making best buy decisions.
* c.   Americans used several different cognitive strategies when making best buy decisions, ranging from more global to more articulated.
  d.   Americans relied exclusively on formal mathematical calculation when making best buy decisions.

19. According to the example from the work of Jean Lave in the text, the difference between the use of mathematics in the supermarket and the use of mathematics in the schoolroom is that
  a.   in the school, problem solvers have no choice but to try to solve problems, and if they choose not to, or do not find the correct answer, they "fail."
  b.   shoppers do not visit supermarkets in order to practice formal mathematical calculation, but this is exactly what schoolroom mathematics exercises are for.
  c.   in the supermarket, problems are dilemmas to be resolved, not problems to be solved.
* d.   all of the above are true

20. Why did Kenge, a Mbuti from Zaire, mistake buffalo for insects?
  a.   They were small buffalo.
  b.   He was seeing them from an airplane.
* c.   He had never seen them from such a great distance.
  d.   Their horns looked like insect antennae.

21. The nexus of relations between the mind at work and the world in which it works is a definition of
  a.   perception.
* b.   cognition.
  c.   rationality.
  d.   intelligence.

22. Rational thinking is best understood as
  a.   learning.
  b.   logic.
  c.   syllogistic reasoning.
* d.   going beyond the information given.

23. The ways in which people understand a cognitive task, encode the information presented to them, and transform that information is
  a.   culturally shaped.
  b.   called a reasoning style.
  c.   found only in formal logic.
* d.   both a and b

24. Which of the following statements about formal logic is false?
  a.   It is a reasoning style that is found in all cultures.
  b.   It is a reasoning style that is context sensitive.
  c.   It is the same as rational thinking.
* d.   All of the above are false.

25. A reasoning style is
* a.   how people work out problems.
  b.   a cultural logic for solving syllogisms.
  c.   a univeral human characteristic that is connected with logic.
  d.   all of the above

26. When the Kpelle are presented with Western-style syllogisms, they may
  a.   interpret them the way they interpret their own riddles.
  b.   seek the most enlightening and informative answer.
  c.   fail to accept context-free analysis.
* d.   all of the above

27. Which of the following statements about emotion is true?
* a.   It is the product of a dialectic between bodily arousal and cognitive interpretation.
  b.   It is generated automatically regardless of the context.
  c.   The same emotions are found in all human societies.
  d.   All members of the same society experience the same emotions in the same contexts.

28. According to the text, why should we experience emotion at all?
* a.   Emotion alerts us to something new and unexpected in our environment.
    b.   Emotion permits us to develop ways of integrating cognition and perception.
    c.   Without emotion, it would be difficult for us to form any attachments.
    d.   Without emotion there is no bodily arousal.

29. The Giriama emotion translated as "grief" contains which of the following characteristics?
    a.   bitterness
    b.   resignation
    c.   sadness
* d.   both a and c

30. Catherine Lutz' study of emotion among Ifaluk people demonstrates that
* a.   social relationships can be talked about through the language of emotions.
    b.   emotions that appear to be quite distinct from Western emotions are similar.
    c.   Ifaluk internal bodily states are distinct from those registered by people in other kinds of environments.
    d.   politics shapes emotions more than do internal bodily states.

31. Which term highlights the ways in which human beings must learn to pattern and adapt their behavior to what is considered appropriate in the society in which they are living?
    a.   enculturation
* b.   socialization
    c.   accommodation
    d.   assimilation

32. Which term highlights the ways in which human beings must learn to pattern and adapt their ways of thinking and feeling to the ways of thinking and feeling considered appropriate in the culture in which they were born?
* a.   enculturation
    b.   socialization
    c.   accommodation
    d.   assimilation

33. Which of the following thinkers developed a theory of personality development that emphasizes the patterning of emotions in early childhood?
* a.   Freud
  b.   Piaget
  c.   Mead
  d.   Vygotsky

34. Which of the following is NOT one of the domains of the personality according to Freud?
  a.   ego
  b.   id
* c.   other
  d.   superego

35. Which of the following thinkers proposed four stages of development in children's reasoning powers?
  a.   Freud
* b.   Piaget
  c.   Mead
  d.   Vygotsky

36. Which of the following thinkers believed that human nature is completed and enhanced, not curtailed or damaged, by socialization and enculturation?
  a.   Piaget
  b.   Mead
  c.   Vygotsky
* d.   both b and c

37. The concept of the zone of proximal development is associated with which of the following thinkers?
  a.   Freud
  b.   Piaget
  c.   Mead
* d   Vygotsky

38. A child cannot tie her own shoes by herself, but if her best friend is there to talk her through it, she can tie them. Which theory accounts for this situation?
  a.   game stage
  b.   socialization/enculturation
  c.   superego development
* d.   zone of proximal development

39. Research on children in Cuba demonstrates that the zone of proximal development is greater for children of mothers with
* a.   higher levels of education who are in the paid work force.
   b.   lower levels of education who are not in the paid work force.
   c.   higher levels of education who are not in the paid work force.
   d.   lower levels of education who are in the paid work force.

40. Carol Gilligan argues that the moral development of boys and girls
   a.   follows a natural developmental path.
   b.   is conditioned by the needs of society at a given moment.
* c.   begins in different sociocultural contexts.
   d.   varies according to the economic position of the parents.

Essay Questions

41. It is difficult enough to identify and measure cognitive capacities in individuals. The difficulty only increases, however, when different groups of human subjects perform differently on the same psychological test. Why?

42. Syllogistic reasoning is enshrined in Western culture as the core of rational thought. But when Cole and Scribner devised logical problems involving syllogistic reasoning and presented them to their Kpelle subjects, the results were surprising. Describe what happened and how the results might best be understood.

43. Metaphor appears squarely at the center of children's growing awareness of the world around them. Discuss.

44. Patricia Greenfield carried out a study among the Wolof of Senegal, West Africa, using sets of pictures mounted on cards. Discuss the results of her research and why they are important.

45. During his fieldwork with the Mbuti, Turnbull took his informant Kenge out of the forest to open grassland. What was Kenge's reaction? How might we account for such a reaction?

46. Discuss the theoretical contributions of Freud, Piaget, and Vygotsky to our understanding of socialization-enculturation.

47. Discuss some of the features involved in the cultural construction of emotion.

48. What is the zone of proximal development? What is the value of this concept for our understanding of socialization-enculturation?

CHAPTER 16

PLAY, ART, MYTH, AND RITUAL

Outline

PLAY

Thinking about Play
Deep Play
Sport

ART

A Definition of Art
Reflecting and Affecting Culture
The Revolutionary Potential of Art

MYTH

Myth as a Charter for Social Action
Myth as a Conceptual Tool

RITUAL

A Definition of Ritual
Ritual as Action
Rites of Passage
Play and Ritual as Complementary

COMBINING PLAY, ART, MYTH, AND RITUAL

Key Terms

play	art	ritual
metacommunication	transformation-	rite of passage
framing	representation	liminality
reflexivity	myths	communitas
deep play	orthodoxy	orthopraxy
sport		

Arguing Anthropology

1. What is the attraction of deep play?

2. Victor Turner suggested that communitas was as important as structure. Do you agree?

Multiple Choice Questions

1. Play is
   a.   consciously adopted.
   b.   pleasurable.
   c.   transformative.
* d.   all of the above

2. According to the text, play is related to which of the following concepts in linguistics and cognition?
   a.   arbitrariness
   b.   displacement
* c.   openness
   d.   prevarication

3. Some scholars have proposed that play is connected with
   a.   developing cognitive and motor skills involving the brain.
   b.   exercise.
   c.   learning.
* d.   all of the above

4. Robert Fagen proposes that play in animals communicates the message
* a.   "all's well."
   b.   "back off."
   c.   "let's cooperate."
   d.   all of the above

5. An implication of Fagen's work on animal play is that selection for play becomes
   a.   part of the genetic makeup of organisms.
   b.   related to the well-being of the animals involved.
* c.   selection for openness.
   d.   impossible; play is learned behavior.

6. In play
   a.   the means justifies the end.
   b.   the end determines the means.
* c.   the end no longer determines the means.
   d.   none of the above.

7. Andrew Miracle points out that for Bolivian Aymara people in crowded situations, joking
   a. enables friends and relatives to separate themselves from outsiders.
   * b. makes a socially unpleasant situation more tolerable.
   c. leads to fights, especially when personal.
   d. is common, but laughter never accompanies it; people laugh when they retell the jokes at home.

8. Metacommunication refers to
   a. communication systems in advanced societies.
   * b. communication about communication.
   c. ordinary communication studied out of context.
   d. such e-mail practices as the sideways smiley faces [for example, :-)].

9. Marking the play frame can be done by
   a. a dog showing its play face.
   b. a referee's whistle.
   c. the phrase "just joking."
   * d. all of the above

10. Because play offers different ways of thinking about everyday life, it is said to be
    a. dangerous.
    b. fun.
    * c. reflexive.
    d. relativistic.

11. Which of the following observations about play is false?
    a. Play is a source of creativity.
    * b. Play is always good.
    c. Play is practice for the real world.
    d. Play can be a source for changing ordinary life.

12. Where humor critical of rulers is censored, such humor
    a. disappears.
    b. is directed into other channels, frequently about animals or magic.
    * c. becomes a form of political resistance.
    d. is taken over by the ruling elite and used for its own purposes.

168

13. Play in which the stakes are so high that, from a utilitarian perspective, it is irrational for anyone to engage in it at all is called
    a.   sport.
    b.   game.
*   c.   deep play.
    d.   ritual.

14. According to Clifford Geertz, the Balinese cockfight is
    a.   about status relationship.
    b.   a Balinese reflection on violence.
    c.   a story the Balinese tell themselves about themselves.
*   d.   all of the above

15. Which of the following statements about sport is true?
    a.   In the world of institutionalized sport, players are working, not playing.
    b.   Sport that has not been institutionalized remains play.
    c.   Even if a sport has become institutionalized, the spectators are still playing.
*   d.   All of the above are true.

16. What happens when a sport is introduced into a culture that had never known it before?
    a.   Nothing; the rules of the sport are fixed and cannot be changed without damaging the sport.
    b.   Nothing; if the people are willing to play the sport, they will play by the rules, especially if there is international competition.
*   c.   The sport is redefined and adjusted to fit the norms and values of the host culture.
    d.   The sport is redefined and adjusted, but only in those elements external to the basics.

17. Which of the following observations describes professional soccer in Brazil?
    a.   Soccer is central to life in Brazil but virtually unknown anywhere else in the world.
    b.   Soccer represents group coordination, division of labor, minute specialization, mechanization, and controlled violence.
*   c.   For many Brazilians, the experience of supporting a soccer team may be their first and perhaps only experience of a loyalty beyond the local community.
    d.   Both a and b are true.

18. The full institutionalization of sport seems to have taken place in
    a.   bands.
    b.   chiefdoms.
    c.   agricultural societies.
*   d.   modern nation-states.

19. The one important exception to the global mass culture of sport is that
    a.   it is always associated with food.
*   b.   it regularly separates women from men.
    c.   it regularly separates blacks from whites.
    d.   none of the above

20. Which of the following play a role in our aesthetic response to a work of
    art?
    a.   Its ability to affect us emotionally plays a role.
    b.   Its form must be a convincing evaluation of the content.
    c.   Its form must be technically perfect in its realization.
*   d.   All of the above are true.

21. Play with form producing some aesthetically successful transformation-
    representation is a definition of
    a.   games.
*   b.   art.
    c.   sport.
    d.   ritual.

22. Which of the following statements accurately reflect the relationship
    between play and art?
    a.   Art is a kind of play.
    b.   Art is play subject to limitations of form and content.
    c.   Art is taken more seriously than pure play, with the result that
           challenges to its rules are far more threatening.
*   d.   All of the above are true.

23. Artists in non-literate societies
    a.   are divorced from everyday life.
    b.   produce work that is more interesting to Western collectors than it is
           to the people in their own societies.
    c.   are similar to Western artists in that they are concerned with art for
           art's sake.
*   d.   work with symbols that are of central importance to their societies.

24. In Western society, art is affected by
   a.　　artists' images of themselves.
   b.　　market factors.
   c.　　the art establishment.
* d.　　all of the above

25. When the Fang evaluated their sculpture for James Fernandez, which of the
    following factors was not of concern to them?
   a.　　the finished or unfinished quality of the object
   b.　　whether or not the quadrants of the work were balanced with one
         another
* c.　　how closely the proportions of the statues resembled the proportions
         of living men
   d.　　both a and b

26. Jane Cowan observes that in northern Greece, dance
* a.　　plays a role in the social construction of gender.
   b.　　is the art form most appreciated by working class people.
   c.　　provides a safe way for women to enjoy themselves without the
         pressure to conform.
   d.　　All of the above are true.

27. When the Kuranko of West Africa tell folktales, they
   a.　　do so to entertain children, and do not take them seriously.
* b.　　encourage ethical discussion by dramatizing uncertainty,
         ambivalence, and ambiguity.
   c.　　do so in order to emphasize the unchanging nature of the social
         world.
   d.　　only do so because anthropologists request it, since traditional
         folktales have ceased to be of any relevance in their lives.

28. Carnival in Brazil
   a.　　has been influenced by the government and the media.
   b.　　gives people an experience of what revolution would be like.
* c.　　provides poor Afro-Brazilians with a chance to criticize the
         government and politics.
   d.　　excludes Afro-Brazilians from participation.

29. Which of the following statements reflects the way anthropologists understand myth?
   a.   Myths are flawed attempts at science or history.
   b.   Myths may justify past action, explain action in the present, or generate future action.
   c.   Myths are tools for overcoming logical contradictions that cannot otherwise be overcome.
* d.   Both b and c are true.

30. Stories whose truth seems self-evident because they integrate personal experiences with a wider set of assumptions about the way the world works are called
   a.   folktales.
   b.   metaphors.
* c.   myths.
   d.   narrative.

31. When myths and related beliefs that are taken to be self-evident truths are highly codified, and deviation from the code is considered a serious matter, we may call this
   a.   liminality.
* b.   orthodoxy.
   c.   orthopraxy.
   d.   ritual.

32. The anthropologist who argued that myths serve as "charters" or "justifications" for present-day social arrangements was
   a.   E. E. Evans-Pritchard.
   b.   Claude Lévi-Strauss.
* c.   Bronislaw Malinowski.
   d.   Victor Turner.

33. The Blue people control access to power among the Grugenach people. In the old days, before time began, the Red people had arrived first on the Island, before the Blue people, but they had married their father's sister's daughters and had so forfeited their rights to power. The Blue people, true to the ways of the ancestors, always married their father's brother's daughters and so displaced the Red people. This case demonstrates myth as
* a.   a social charter.
   b.   history.
   c.   a conceptual tool.
   d.   flawed history.

34. The anthropologist who argued that myths are tools for overcoming logical contradictions that cannot otherwise be overcome was
   a.   E. E. Evans-Pritchard.
* b.   Claude Lévi-Strauss.
   c.   Bronislaw Malinowski.
   d.   Victor Turner.

35. Which of the following does not reflect the anthropological understanding of ritual?
* a.   Rituals are exclusively religious in nature.
   b.   Rituals are repetitive social practices composed of a sequence of symbolic activities.
   c.   Through ritual performance, the ideas of a culture take on a concrete form.
   d.   Ritual aims to shape action as well as thought, to orient all human faculties in the socially approved direction.

36. Which of the following is learned at a child's birthday party in the United States?
   a.   Exchanging material objects is important in defining significant social relations.
   b.   how to symbolize friendship and sociability
   c.   how to share with other people
* d.   All of the above are true.

37. In ritual, what is the connection of the ritual performance and the ritual text?
   a.   The text determines the performance.
* b.   The text and the performance shape each other.
   c.   In the long run, the performance is more significant than the text.
   d.   The text and the performance are both fixed.

38. The movement to ritual is based on the premise of
   a.   metaphor.
   b.   "Let's make-believe."
* c.   "Let's believe."
   d.   both a and b

39. What are the three stages of rites of passage?
* a.   separation, transition, reaggregation
   b.   effacement, transition, delivery
   c.   liberty, equality, fraternity
   d.   communitas, liminality, marginality

40. An intense comradeship in which the social distinctions among participants in a ritual disappear or become irrelevant is called
    a.   liminality.
*   b.   communitas.
    c.   transition.
    d.   reaggregation.

41. "Liminal," from the Latin word "limen" means
    a.   sprite.
    b.   containing.
    c.   transporting.
*   d.   threshold.

42. Play communicates about _____; ritual communicates about
    _____.
    a.   body; mind
    b.   what should be; what is
*   c.   what can be; what ought to be
    d.   what is; what will be

43. When nearly every act of everyday life is ritualized and other forms of behavior are strongly proscribed, the term used is
    a.   liminality.
    b.   orthodoxy.
*   c.   orthopraxy.
    d.   ritual.

44 The demon exorcism of the Sinhalese Buddhists studied by Bruce Kapferer had which of the following features?
*   a.   It lasted all night.
    b.   Its purpose was to purify a household prior to the wedding of one of its members.
    c.   It was performed only for members of the ruling class.
    d.   All of the above are true.

45. In the Sinhalese Buddhist demon exorcism ritual,
    a.   the beginning comedy puts the audience at ease and is then followed by a serious dramatic performance.
    b.   the beginning action is the incorporation of audience and patient into the serious and threatening reality in which the gods dominate.
*   c.   when comedy begins, the demons are turned into figures of ridicule, allowing the gods to reappear and assert their dominance.
    d.   the success of the ritual depends on the ability of patient and audience to remain completely serious from beginning to end.

174

Essay Questions

46. Metacommunication places cognitive boundaries, or frames, around certain behaviors and says that they are "play" or that they are "ordinary life." Discuss, using examples.

47. Discuss the significance of taking play seriously. What effect does this have on our understanding of human culture? In your answer, be sure to define play and discuss its connections with other aspects of the human experience.

48. "Play is only one component of sport." Do you agree or disagree with this statement? Defend your choice with examples.

49. "Play is not always good." What does this statement mean? Illustrate your answer with examples.

50. What is meant by the suggestion that play is a form of art? In what ways does art differ from pure play?

51. Is art a universal language? Why or why not?

52. Describe what is meant by "transformation-representation." How does this concept help anthropologists discuss art from a cross-cultural perspective?

53. Using two or three examples, discuss the ways in which art reflects and affects culture.

54. Sports in the United States (and elsewhere) have become big business and big politics. Does this represent a corruption of originally untainted activities that we could eliminate if we had the will, or is it a virtually inevitable outcome of life in a modern nation-state? Discuss, illustrating your answer with examples.

55. Discuss the two ways of understanding myth considered in the text. What are the strengths and weaknesses of each position? Are they mutually contradictory?

56. What are the stages of rites of passage? Define each one and give concrete examples.

57. People in a liminal state tend to develop communitas. Why is this so?

58. What are the connections among play, art, myth, and ritual? Give examples.

CHAPTER 17

WORLDVIEW

Outline

Key Terms

worldviews
metaphors
metaphorical subject
metaphorical predicate
metaphorical entailments
metonymy
symbol

witchcraft
magic
oracles
key metaphors
societal metaphor
organic metaphor
technological metaphor

computer metaphor
religion
shaman
priest
syncretism
revitalization

Arguing Anthropology

1. What makes a worldview compelling?

2. In one of the In Their Own Words selections in this chapter, Andrea Smith writes, "When everyone becomes 'Indian,' then it is easy to lose sight of the specificity of oppression faced by those who are Indian in this lfie. It is no wonder we have such a difficult time finding non-Indians to support our struggles when the New Age movement has completely disguised our oppression." What does she mean? Do you agree?

Multiple Choice Questions

1. Encompassing pictures of reality created by the members of a particular society are called
   a. schemas.
   b. experiential gestalts.
* c. world views.
   d. metaphors.

2. In the phrase "He who lives by the sword dies by the sword," the word "sword" is a _____, representing the domain of violence.
* a. metonym
   b. metaphorical subject
   c. metaphorical predicate
   d. simile

3. The phrase "My soul is an eagle" is an example of
   a. metonym.
* b. metaphor.
   c. simile.
   d. entailment.

4. Symbols may be
   a. words.
   b. images.
   c. actions.
* d. all of the above

5. To many people, the American flag stands for "the American way." The flag is thus an example of
   a. an elaborating symbol.
* b. a summarizing symbol.
   c. a personal symbol.
   d. an archetype.

6. Which of the following represents for members of a society, in an emotionally powerful way, what their way of life means to them?
   a.   elaborating symbols
* b.   summarizing symbols
   c.   personal symbols
   d.   national symbols

7. According to Godfrey Lienhardt, the Dinka use cattle as
* a.   elaborating symbols.
   b.   summarizing symbols.
   c.   personal symbols.
   d.   archetypes.

8. Which of the following are analytic, providing people with categories for thinking about the order of the world?
* a.   elaborating symbols
   b.   summarizing symbols
   c.   personal symbols
   d.   national symbols

9. The Azande use chicken for
   a.   stir fry.
   b.   celebrations.
* c.   detecting witches.
   d.   enhancing the powers of witchcraft.

10. For the Azande, witchcraft
    a.   consists of spells that must be purchased from other witches.
    b.   is a substance in the body of witches.
    c.   is ordinarily practised by women.
    d.   is most powerful in important chiefs.

11. To the Azande, witches are
    a.   neighbors.
    b.   anti-social.
    c.   those whose behavior is out of line.
    d.   all of the above

12. When Azande believe they have been victimized by witchcraft, their usual response is
    a.   fear.
*   b.   anger.
    c.   to run to the chief to ask for protection.
    d.   to suspect the chief of being a witch.

13. For the Azande, deaths are caused by
    a.   natural causes, old age, and witchcraft.
    b.   old age and witchcraft.
    c.   natural causes and old age.
*   d.   witchcraft.

14. An invisible force to which the Azande address questions and whose reponses they believe to be truthful is called
    a.   a witch.
    b.   a magician.
*   c.   an oracle.
    d.   a chief.

15. Witchcraft beliefs, especially witchcraft accusations
    a.   can serve to unify a society.
    b.   can defend the wider values of a community.
    c.   can weaken in-group ties.
*   d.   all of the above

16. Accusations of witchcraft reaffirm group boundaries and solidarity when
*   a.   the accused is an outsider.
    b.   the accused is an insider.
    c.   the accused is a woman.
    d.   All of the above are true.

17. Accusations of witchcraft realign factions within a society when
    a.   the accused is an outsider.
*   b.   the accused is an insider.
    c.   the accused is a man.
    d.   All of the above are true.

18. "The web of life" is an example of
    a.   a societal metaphor.
*   b.   an organic metaphor.
    c.   a technological metaphor.
    d.   a conduit metaphor.

19. "He's a real ROM (read only memory) head" is an example of a
a.   conduit metaphor.
b.   organic metaphor.
c.   societal metaphor.
* d.   computer metaphor.

20. Robin Horton suggests that people who construct a world view are concerned above all to show that the world is
* a.   orderly and predictable.
b.   changing and unpredictable.
c.   peopled with invisible superhuman beings.
d.   empty of supernatural forces.

21. How can metaphors, or the symbols that represent them, be used as instruments of power?
a.   when they are under the direct control of a person wishing to affect the behavior of others
b.   when they are used for reference or in support of certain conduct
c.   when some people are able to impose their metaphors on others
* d.   All of the above are true.

22. According to Mary Douglas, the ancient Hebrews interpreted threats to society as if they were
a.   threats against God.
b.   threats against their king alone.
* c.   threats to the body.
d.   threats to national sovereignty.

23. Which of the following is entailed by the conduit metaphor?
a.   Ideas are objects.
b.   Linguistic expressions are containers.
c.   Communication is sending.
* d.   All of the above are true.

24. Syncretism involves
a.   discarding the old ways and embracing the new.
b.   resisting the new ways and defending the old.
c.   combining the old and the new in an attempt to cope with changed circumstances.
d.   inventing a way of life that has nothing to do with the old or the new.

25. Nativism refers to
a.   going native.
* b.   ridding society of alien influences.
c.   following a messiah to a new golden age.
d.   none of the above

26. When the President of the United States says, "Americans are waging a war on poverty", what is the underlying metaphor?
a.   Poverty is the enemy.
b.   The citizens of the United States are an army.
c.   There will be many casualties.
* d.   Both a and b are true.

27. Gods, spirits, oracles, and witchcraft substance are all alike in that
a.   they can be addressed in human language.
b.   they are expected to respond to human beings in terms we can understand.
c.   they can be found in societies whose members conceive of cosmic forces in terms of a societal metaphor.
* d.   All of the above are true.

28. If people construct a world view in terms of a societal metaphor, this is because (according to Robin Horton) they associate the social world with
a.   constant, unpredictable change.
* b.   order, regularity, and predictability.
c.   spirituality.
d.   materialism.

29. When contemporary sociobiologists describe the nurturing behavior of parents toward their offspring as "parental investment," they are using what kind of metaphor?
a.   economic
b.   societal
c.   technological
* d.   both a and b

30. When the characteristics of human beings are attributed to non-human entities, this is an example of
a.   a technological metaphor.
b.   an organic metaphor.
c.   personification.
* d.   both b and c

31. The growth of Western science and technology contributed to the rise of which of the following kinds of key metaphor?
   a.   societal
* b.   technological
   c.   organic
   d.   religious

32. Which of the following is NOT a minimal category of religion, according to Anthony F. C. Wallace?
   a.   music
   b.   reciting the code
* c.   reflexiveness
   d.   simulation

33. The principle that sacred things are to be touched so that power may be transferred refers to which of the following minimal categories of religion?
   a.   prayer
   b.   simulation
* c.   mana
   d.   taboo

34. Every religious system in the world has a customary way of addressing the supernatural. This feature is captured by the minimal category of religion called
* a.   prayer.
   b.   exhortation.
   c.   reciting the code.
   d.   taboo.

35. In some religious systems, certain individuals may become possessed or undergo some other form of religious ecstasy. This is captured in the minimal category of religion called
   a.   physiological exercise.
   b.   mana.
   c.   sacrifice.
* d.   inspiration.

36. Part-time religious practitioners who are believed to have the power to contact supernatural forces directly are called
* a.   shamans.
   b.   priest.
   c.   oracles.
   d.   witches.

37. Religious specialists skilled in the practice of religious rituals, which they carry out for the benefit of the group, are called
   a.   shamans.
* b.   priests.
   c.   oracles.
   d.   witches.

38. For the Huichol, the three key symbols of life in Wirikuta are
   a.   witchcraft, oracles, and magic.
   b.   magic, science, and religion.
* c.   deer, maize, and peyote.
   d.   chicken, fire, and water.

39. According to Barbara Myerhoff, the Huichol explain present-day moral incoherence by
   a.   asserting that following an ancient sin, an original paradise was lost.
   b.   asserting that there is an afterlife in which all the suffering of the world will be set right.
* c.   regaining an idealized past and integrating it into the present.
   d.   maintaining a sense of control over chaos through the practice of vengeance magic.

40. According to James Fernandez, Bwiti cult groups often split apart when
   a.   members refuse to make explicit the entailments of key metaphors.
* b.   leaders disagree over the aptness of certain metaphors and of the rituals that follow from them.
   c.   the government withdraws financial support of public rituals.
   d.   Christian missionaries become established in an area.

Essay Questions

41. Why did magic fail to return the stolen bicycle as described in the story that opens the chapter? Be sure to include Amadou's explanation as well as that of the anthropologists.

42. In many societies, the model for the wider world is the social order. Discuss the consequences that follow from this and illustrate with examples.

43. What are some consequences that follow from drawing the key metaphors of a world view from technology? Illustrate with examples.

44. What are the three ways in which metaphoric innovation can proceed? Discuss each and illustrate with an example.

45. Summarize the interrelationship of witchcraft, oracles, and magic for the Azande. What is the logic of the system from an Azande perspective? How would a nonbelieving outsider explain its workings? Can you think of any tests whose outcome could be used to verify or falsify either interpretation?

46. What is a revitalization movement? What forms can it take? Illustrate with examples.

47. Why is the concept of metaphor so important to an analysis of world view in anthropology?

48. Discuss the relationship between world view and power. Illustrate your answer with examples.

49. What is a key metaphor? Choose two of the key metaphors discussed in the text and discuss the kinds of entailments that follow from them once a world view is based on them.

50. On what grounds is an anthropologist justified in calling the peyote hunt of the Huichol of Mexico a religious activity? Discuss.

CHAPTER 18

KINSHIP

Outline

KINSHIP SYSTEMS: WAYS OF ORGANIZING HUMAN
INTERDEPENDENCE

Determining Group Membership and Relationships
Sex, Gender, and Kinship
Understanding Different Kinship Systems

PATTERNS OF DESCENT IN KINSHIP

Bilateral Kindreds
Unilineal Descent Groups

LINEAGES

Lineage Membership
The Logic of Lineage Relationships
Patrilineages
Matrilineages

KINSHIP TERMINOLOGIES

Criteria for Distinctions
Pattersns of Kinship Terminology

KINSHIP AND ALLIANCE THROUGH MARRIAGE

INDIGENOUS VIEWS OF KINSHIP

KINSHIP EXTENDED: LITERALAND METAPHORICAL KIN

Negotiation among the Ju/'hoansi (!Kung)
European-American Kinship and New Reproductive Technologies
Compadrazgo in Latin America
Ie in Contemporary Japan
Kinship as Metaphor

KINSHIP AND PRACTICE

KINSHIP: A FRAMEWORK FOR INTERPRETING LIFE

Key Terms

kinship	patrilineage	bifurcation
marriage	matrilineage	parallel cousins
descent	lineages	cross cousins
sex	clan	direct exchange marriage
gender	segmentary opposition	asymmetrical exchange
bilateral descent	bridewealth	marriage
unilineal descent	affinity	*compadrazgo*
bilateral kindred	collaterality	consanguineal

Arguing Anthropology

1. How does adoption fit into the American theory of kinship? Are adoptive parents "really" parents, or are they something else?

2. In what ways might "blended families," single-parent families by choice, or nonreproductive sexual relationships affect kinship patterns in a given society?

Multiple Choice Questions

1. Which of the following observations about kinship is stressed by the authors of the text?
   a. Different societies have chosen to highlight some features of the universal human experiences of mating and birth while downplaying or ignoring others.
   b. Kinship is reducible to biology.
   c. Both matrilineal descent and patrilineal descent can be defended with reference to the universal human experiences of mating and birth.
 * d. Both a and c are true.

2. In addition to establishing links between generations through descent, kinship serves to establish
   a. legitimacy of children.
   b. residence rules.
   c. inheritance patterns.
 * d. all of the above

3. When Martha Macintyre went to do fieldwork on the island of Tubetube in Papua New Guinea, what happened when she found that the only person who could translate for her was a young married man?
   a. She was made into his fictive "wife" to avoid scandal.
 * b. She was made into his fictive "elder sister" to avoid scandal.
   c. She accepted the status of "sinabada," or "senior white woman," to avoid scandal.
   d. She had to move to a different village to find a female translator who could work with her without creating a scandal.

4. The study of kinship became important in anthropology because
   a. kinship could be reduced to biology and thus could make cross-cultural comparison objective.
   b. it showed how people could maintain social order without the institution of the state.
   c. it enabled anthropologists to explain why some societies had remained primitive and others had advanced.
   d. kinship no longer existed in Western societies.

5. The North American kinship term *aunt* refers to
   a.   a woman who occupies a unique biological position.
   b.   a woman who may be related to us in one of two different ways.
* c.   a woman who may be related to us in one of four different ways.
   d.   a kin category that is recognized in all human kinship systems.

6. The central person around which any kinship diagram is organized is known as
* a.   ego.
   b.   cross cousin.
   c.   parallel cousin.
   d.   mother's brother's daughter.

7. Kinship relationships derived from mating are called
   a.   descent.
* b   marriage.
   c.   patrilineal.
   d.   matrilineal.

8. Kinship relationships based on birth are called
* a.   descent.
   b.   marriage.
   c.   prescriptive.
   d.   generational.

9. Which of the following terms do anthropologists use to refer to the observable physical characteristics that distinguish the two kinds of human beings, male and female, needed for human biological reproduction?
* a.   sex
   b.   gender
   c.   hermaphroditism
   d.   berdache

10. Which of the following terms do anthropologists use to refer to the cultural construction of beliefs and behaviors considered appropriate for males and females in a particular society?
   a.   sex
* b.   gender
   c.   hermaphroditism
   d.   berdache

11. The phenomenon called guevedoche ("penis at twelve") in the Dominican Republic is
a.   the same as the indigenous North American phenomenon called berdache.
b.   involves an irregularity in the pattern of X and Y chromosomes.
* c.   is due to a hormonal defect that causes children to be born with ambiguous genitals.
d.   is a result of the deliberate castration of chromosomal males at puberty.

12. Eunuchs in the Byzantine civilization of late antiquity are an example of
a.   a supernumerary sex based on the presence of ambiguous genitals at birth.
* b.   a supernumerary sex that was deliberately created by destroying or removing a male's testicles before puberty.
c.   a supernumerary sex based on the surgical removal of genitalia on adult males.
d.   a supernumerary gender role that apparently had nothing to do with morphological sex anomalies.

13. The hijras of Gujarat, India are an example of
a.   a supernumerary sex based on the presence of ambiguous genitals at birth.
b.   a supernumerary sex that was deliberately created by destroying or removing a male's testicles before puberty.
* c.   a supernumerary sex based on the surgical removal of genitalia on adult males.
d.   a supernumerary gender role that apparently had nothing to do with morphological sex anomalies.

14. The berdache of many indigenous North American societies is an example of
a.   a supernumerary sex based on the presence of ambiguous genitals at birth.
b.   a supernumerary sex that was deliberately created by destroying or removing a male's testicles before puberty.
c.   a supernumerary sex based on the surgical removal of genitalia on adult males.
* d.   a supernumerary gender role that apparently had nothing to do with morphological sex anomalies.

15. According to Will Roscoe, the presence of multiple genders requires
a. a belief in the existence of three or more physical sexes.
b. a view of physical differences as unfixed or insufficient on their own to establish gender.
c. a view of physical differences as simply less important that individual or social factors in determining gender.
* d. both b or c to be true.

16. Gilbert Herdt's survey of the ethnographic literature leads him to conclude that
a. it is easy for a society to maintain supernumerary sexes or genders.
* b. it is difficult for a society to maintain supernumerary sexes or genders.
c. it is harder for a society to maintain supernumerary sexes that it is to maintain supernumerary genders.
d. supernumerary sexes and genders are never found alongside strongly marked male-female duality.

17. Among the Sambia of New Guinea,
a. male-female duality was unimportant.
b. male-female duality was strongly marked.
c. a supernumerary sex was found.
* d. both b and c are true.

18. According to Gilbert Herdt, a strong case can be made for the existence of a supernumerary sex or gender if
a. children in the society are born with ambiguous genitals.
b. chromosomally normal males are found performing female tasks, and chromosomally normal females are found performing male tasks.
* c. a culture defines for each sex or gender a symbolic niche and a social pathway of development into later life that is distinctly different from the cultural life plan set out by a model based on male/female duality.
d. Both a and b are true.

19. Matrilineages have long been misunderstood by Westerners because we assume
a. the existence of male dominance.
b. the existence of hierarchy.
c. that women never have social power.
* d. all of the above

20. A unilineage can be
a.   matrilineal.
b.   cognatic.
c.   bilateral.
* d.   both b and c

21. A kindred is composed of
a.   those people linked to Ego through men only.
* b.   those people linked to Ego through Ego's mother and Ego's father.
c.   those people linked to Ego on the father's side only.
d.   everyone related to Ego by consanguinity and affinity.

22. Kinship terminologies suggest
a.   the boundaries of the significant groups in the society.
b.   where cleavages within groups are likely to occur.
c.   the structure of rights and obligations assigned to different members of the society.
* d.   All of the above are true.

23. The kinship tie created by marriage is called
a.   collaterality.
b.   bifurcation.
* c.   affinity.
d.   consanguinity.

24. The kinship tie created by birth is called
a.   collaterality.
b.   bifurcation.
c.   affinity.
* d.   consanguinity.

25. The distinction made between kin who are believed to be in a direct line and those who are off to one side is called
* a.   collaterality.
b.   bifurcation.
c.   affinity.
d.   consanguinity.

26. The distinction made between the mother's side of the family and the father's side of the family is called
  a.   collaterality.
* b.   bifurcation.
  c.   affinity.
  d.   consanguinity.

27. The pattern of kinship terminology based on the criteria of generation and sex alone is called
  a.   Eskimo.
  b.   Sudanese.
* c.   Hawaiian.
  d.   Crow.

28. The Eskimo pattern of kinship terminology
  a.   isolates the nuclear family.
  b.   is also the American pattern of kinship terminology.
  c.   pays no attention to generation once the immediate collateral line is considered.
* d.   all of the above

29. Merging the mother's and father's parallel siblings with the parents is typical of which system of kinship terminology?
  a.   Crow
  b.   Omaha
* c.   Iroquois
  d.   Sudanese

30. Among the Ju/'hoansi (!Kung), every individual in the society can be linked to every other individual by
  a.   residence.
  b.   lineage membership.
  c.   friendship and cooperative work groups.
* d.   a kinship term.

31. For the Ju/'hoansi (!Kung), kinship connections are
  a.   negotiated.
  b.   manipulated through the principle of wi.
  c.   continually changing over the course of a lifetime.
* d.   all of the above

32. Which of the following are not matrilineal societies?
a. Iroquois
b. Crow
c. Navajo
* d. Omaha

33. What happens if a male Ego lives in a society practicing asymmetrical exchange marriage, and his mother's brother does not have a daughter?
a. He remains unmarried.
b. His mother's brother is forced to adopt a daughter of marriageable age.
c. He is forced to emigrate.
* d. There is no real difficulty, since it is not necessary that he marry a literal mother's brother's daughter, just an appropriate woman born to a man of his mother's lineage.

34. The term "fictive kin" may refer to
a. metaphoric kinship.
b. co-parenthood or *compadrazgo*.
c. adoption.
* d. all of the above

35. Western explorers discovered that some nonWestern people use the same kin term to refer to father and father's brother. They did this because
a. they did not know who their real fathers were.
* b. in their society, father and father's brother had the same social significance.
c. they practiced group marriage.
d. both a and c are true.

36. Which of the following distinguishes a bilateral kindred from a lineage?
* a. Kindreds have overlapping memberships, whereas lineages do not.
b. Lineages are descent groups, whereas kindreds are not.
c. Membership in a kindred is traced through only one parent, whereas membership in a lineage is traced through both parents.
d. Membership in a kindred is traced through females, whereas membership in lineages is traced through males.

37. Among the Nuer, if a quarrel erupted between members of different minor lineages, it would ordinarily be resolved when the quarreling minor lineages recognized that they were all part of the same major lineage. This process is called
   a.   lineality.
* b.   segmentary opposition.
   c.   the patrilineal puzzle.
   d.   clanship.

38. The expression "patrilineal puzzle" refers to which of the following situations?
   a.   Men live with their mother's brothers but inherit from their fathers.
* b.   Women who are not lineage members are relied upon to produce the children who perpetuate the lineage.
   c.   Men who are not lineage members are relied upon to produce the children who perpetuate the lineage.
   d.   Men inherit from their mother's brothers but live with their fathers.

39. The expression "matrilineal puzzle" refers to which of the following situations?
   a.   Men live with their mother's brothers, but inherit from their fathers.
   b.   Women who are not lineage members are relied upon to produce the children who perpetuate the lineage.
   c.   Men who are not lineage members are relied upon to produce the children who perpetuate the lineage.
* d.   Men inherit from their mother's brothers but live with their fathers.

40. In the vocabulary of kinship studies, father's brother's children or mother's sister's children are called
* a.   parallel cousins.
   b.   cross cousins.
   c.   first cousins.
   d.   second cousins.

41. In the vocabulary of kinship studies, father's sister's children and mother's brother's children are called
   a.   parallel cousins.
* b.   cross cousins.
   c.   first cousins.
   d.   second cousins.

42. Which of the following features characterizes Crow and Omaha kinship terminologies?
   a.   Both are found in societies that trace descent matrilineally.
   b.   Both are found in societies that trace descent patrilineally.
* c.   In both, lineage membership is more important than generation for grouping together certain relatives.
   d.   Both a and c are true.

43. Among the people of Mount Hagen, New Guinea, women are distinguished from men of their own clan and from men of their husband's clan because
   a.   women move away from their own clans when they marry.
   b.   women carry their clan identity with them when they move.
   c.   women are seen as both connected and disconnected at the same time.
* d.   All of the above are true.

44. In late twentieth century Euroamerican society, the term "natural parent" has come to refer to
   a.   someone who is the unmarried biological parent of a child.
   b.   someone who donates sperm or ova for assisted reproduction.
* c.   someone who is both the biological and the social parent of a child.
   d.   someone who is a child's caregiver, but was not biologically responsible for engendering the child in question.

45. According to Marilyn Strathern, the new reproductive technologies make clear that, in Euroamerican societies,
   a.   kinship relations remain nonnegotiable.
   b.   even the world of natural facts is subject to social intervention.
   c.   kinship relations are negotiable.
* d.   both b and c

46. In the Latin American practice of ritual coparenthood called *compradrazgo*, the most important relationship is between
   a.   the baptized child and its godparents.
* b.   the parents of the baptized child and the child's godparents.
   c.   the baptized child and the children of its godparents.
   d.   the parents of the baptized child and the godparents' children.

47. Which of the following statements describes the *ie* in contemporary Japan?
   a.   Blood relationship is only one method of membership recruitment.
   b.   It is a unit of production based on social and economic ties.
   c.   The core of the *ie* may be composed of people who are not necessarily related biologically.
* d.   All of the above are true.

48. In order to assure continuity of the *ie* from one generation to the next,
a.   two permanent members related by blood must be recruited.
b.   members prefer succession by the youngest son.
* c.   a married couple, unrelated to group members, may be adopted by the *ie*.
d.   the successors to the present leaders are adopted when young and inherit from their adoptive parents.

49. According to Ivan Karp, a Teso man who lives apart from other members of his patrilineage
a.   can rely on his mother's relatives to handle the funeral of one of his children.
b.   can be buried in the territory of either his paternal or maternal kin.
* c.   may find himself open to a lack of support in a crisis.
d.   both a and b

50. The Ilongot experience of kinship shows that
a.   kinship rules offer tried-and-true formulas for resolving every dilemma
b.   a social order based on kinship has little flexibility from one generation to the next.
* c.   resolutions of conflicting demands by different categories of kin must be worked out in the context of the situations in which actors find themselves.
d.   it makes more sense to favor affinal ties and to downplay consanguineal ties, when the two conflict.

Essay Questions

51. Describe the Hawaiian kinship system. Which of its features led Westerners to misinterpret it, and why?

52. What does it mean to say that lineage organization can function as the foundation of social life? Give examples.

53. What are the "puzzles" that lie at the heart of patrilineal and matrilineal descent?

54. Compare matrilineality with patrilineality. How are they similar? How are they different? Give examples.

55. Americans tend to think that kinship mirrors biology. What do such kin terms as "aunt," "uncle," and "cousin" suggest about the cultural construction of the American kinship system?

56. What are the seven criteria most often drawn upon in the construction of kinship terminologies? Illustrate each with an example.

57. Kinship is based upon, but not reducible, to biology. Give evidence to support this assertion.

58. What are the differences between bilateral and unilineal kinship systems?

59. Richard Lee (1984,57), discussing Ju/'hoansi (!Kung) kinship, writes, "The principles of kinship constitute, not an invariant code of laws written in stone, but instead a whole series of codes, consistent enough to provide structure but open enough to be flexible. I found the best way to look at !Kung kinship is as a game, full of ambiguity and nuance." Do you agree with Lee's appraisal of !Kung kinship? Does Lee's comment apply to other kinship systems you have read about? Discuss.

CHAPTER 19

MARRIAGE AND THE FAMILY

Outline

TOWARD A DEFINITION OF MARRIAGE?

Nuer Woman Marriage
Nuer Ghost Marriage

MARRIAGE AS A SOCIAL PROCESS

Patterns of Residence after Marriage
Single and Plural Spouses
Polyandry, Sexuality, and the Reproductive Capacity of Women
Inuit Comarriage

BRIDEWEALTH

Bridewealth in Southern Africa: Linking Brothers and Sisters

BROTHERS AND SISTERS IN CROSS-CULTURAL PERSPECTIVE

Brothers and Sisters in a Matrilineal Society
Brothers and Sisters in a Patrilineal Society

FAMILY STRUCTURE

The Nuclear Family
The Polygynous Family
Extended and Joint Families

TRANSFORMATIONS IN FAMILIES OVER TIME

Divorce and Remarriage
Breaking up Complex Households
International Migration and the Family

THE FLEXIBILITY OF MARRIAGE

SEXUAL PRACTICES

Ranges of Heterosexual Practices
Nonreproductive Sexual Practices

SEX, MARRIAGE, AND POWER

Key Terms

marriage	patrilocal	polyandry
affinal	matrilocal	bridewealth
consanguineal	avunculocal	nuclear family
endogamy	monogamy	extended family
exogamy	polygamy	joint family
neolocal	polygny	

Arguing Anthropology

1. Marriages in a number of places in the world today continue to be arranged, sometimes by families, sometimes by professional matchmakers. Many people raised in western European or North American contexts find this hard to imagine. What are the advantages or arranged marriages?

2. Sometimes, early in marriage, a North American spouse may blurt out, "Who did I marry, anyway, you or your family?" What could lead to such a remark and how could it be considered naive?

Multiple Choice Questions

1. Which of the following may be considered a prototypical criterion of marriage?
    a.   It involves a man and a woman.
    b.   It stipulates the degree of sexual access allowed the partners.
    c.   It creates ties between the kin of the bride and the kin of the groom.
*   d.   All of the above are true.

2. Which of the following does not involve a transformation in the status of both the parties involved and any offspring produced?
    a.   monogamy
    b.   polygyny
*   c.   mating
    d.   marriage

3. For woman marriage to be possible, a society must recognize a distinction between
    a.   wife and prostitute.
    b.   father and father's brother.
    c.   heterosexuality and homosexuality.
*   d.   pater and genitor.

4. Woman marriage among the Nuer is an example of
    a.   ritual homosexuality.
    b.   mating.
*   c.   what can happen when the role of husband and father is independent of the sex of the person carrying out the role.
    d.   what happens in a society where women outnumber men.

5. Following a marriage, the kin of the husband and the kin of the wife are linked by
* a. affinity.
  b. consanguinity.
  c. endogamy.
  d. exogamy.

6. Marriage patterns that require individuals to find spouses within the boundaries of their own group are called
  a. affinal.
  b. consanguineal.
* c. endogamous.
  d. exogamous.

7. Marriage patterns that require individuals to find spouses outside the boundaries of their own group are called
  a. affinal.
  b. consanguineal.
  c. endogamous.
* d. exogamous.

8. The postmarital residence rule requiring a couple to live with, or near, the husband's mother's brother is called
  a. patrilocal.
  b. matrilocal.
* c. avunculocal.
  d. neolocal.

9. The postmarital residence rule requiring a couple to live with, or near, the husband's father is called
* a. patrilocal.
  b. matrilocal.
  c. avunculocal.
  d. neolocal.

10. The incest taboo
  a. forbids marriage between certain people.
  b. forbids mating between certain people.
  c. differs in scope from one society to another.
* d. all of the above

11. The postmarital residence rule requiring a couple to live with, or near, the wife's mother is called
   a.   patrilocal.
* b.   matrilocal.
   c.   avunculocal.
   d.   neolocal.

12. A form of marriage in which a person may have several spouses is called
   a.   monogamy.
* b.   polygamy.
   c.   exogamy.
   d.   endogamy.

13. A spousal pattern in which a woman may have multiple husbands is called
   a.   polygamy.
   b.   polygyny.
* c.   polyandry.
   d.   all of the above

14. Marriage patterns
* a.   reveal differences in the culturally shaped understanding of male and female sexuality.
   b.   are a function of the urgency of male sexual desire.
   c.   universally subordinate females to males.
   d.   both b and c

15. Which of the following spousal patterns resemble one another in that they control women's sexuality much more closely than they control men's sexuality?
   a.   exogamy and endogamy
   b.   monogamy and polyandry
* c.   monogamy and polygyny
   d.   polygyny and polyandry

16. Which of the following spousal patterns depends upon recognition of a distinction between a women's sexuality and her reproductive capacity?
   a.   monogamy
   b.   polygamy
   c.   polygyny
* d.   polyandry

17. Polyandry is found in which of the following regions of the world?
a.   Tibet and Nepal
b.   South India and Sri Lanka
c.   Northern Nigeria and Northern Cameroon
* d.   all of the above

18. The form of polyandry in which a woman may marry men who are not brothers is called
a.   fraternal polyandry.
* b.   associated polyandry.
c.   polygynandry.
d.   none of the above

19. Polyandry may serve to concentrate relationships among already associated lineages. This practice is called
* a.   alliance intensifying.
b.   alliance proliferative.
c.   alliance abortive.
d.   none of the above

20. In Guider, Muslim women can escape from marriage by
a.   engaging in secondary marriage.
b.   petitioning local authorities to grant her a divorce.
* c.   making her husband's life so unpleasant that he grants her a divorce.
d.   none of the above; in Guider, divorce is impossible.

21. In ancient Rome, divorce was impossible because
a.   at marriage, a woman lost her membership in the patrilineage into which she was born.
b.   at marriage, a woman was incorporated into the lineage of her husband.
c.   the Romans always married within the boundaries of a clan, so that husbands and wives could never cut the kinship ties that bound them to each other.
* d.   both a and b

22. Which of the following statements describes divorce among the Ju/'hoansi (!Kung)?
a.   Divorce was impossible.
b.   Divorce was possible only if husbands repaid the bridewealth in full.
c.   Divorce was possible only if no children had been born to the married couple.
* d.   Mutual consent was all that was required for divorce to occur.

23. Which of the following statements describes divorce among the Inuit?
   a.   Divorce was impossible.
   b.   Married partners who had been living apart could reactivate their marriage simply by beginning to live together again.
   c.   When a married couple split up, and the partners remarried, the consequence was more, not fewer, affinal connections.
* d.   All of the above are true.

24. Which of the following statements describes the migrant families from the Dominican Republic studied by Eugenia Georges?
   a.   The most common pattern was for nuclear families with small children to migrate to New York together.
   b.   Usually, wives went to New York first while their husbands stayed in the Dominican Republic.
* c.   Usually, husbands went to New York first while their wives stayed in the Dominican Republic.
   d.   It was rare for any of the migrants to New York to try to bring other relatives to stay with them there.

25. In Georges' study, what was the most typical way in which the migration cycle from the Dominican Republic to New York ended?
   a.   The husbands in New York broke off ties to their families in the Dominican Republic and never returned.
   b.   Husbands brought wives and children to live with them in New York, where they all settled permanently.
   c.   Husbands occasionally returned to the Dominican Republic, but wives and children usually refused to return once they were settled in New York.
* d.   After several years in the United States, the married couple who started the migration cycle would take their savings and return home to the Dominican Republic.

26. Which of the following statements describes the way migrants from Los Pinos handled the burden of separation from their families in the Dominican Republic?
   a.   The burden eventually grew so heavy that husbands stopped writing or telephoning their families, leaving their wives and children in Los Pinos on their own.
* b.   The burden of separation was lightened by frequent communication, by visiting, and by the continued role of husband as breadwinner and main decision-maker.
   c.   The divorce rate in migrant families was much higher than the divorce rate in families that remained in Los Pinos.
   d.   Both a and c are true.

27. Which of the following cultural beliefs reinforce the practice of polyandry by the Nyinba?
   a.   a tradition that their ancestors, who practiced monogamy, were cursed with lives of disharmony
* b.   a kinship ideal stressing the solidarity of brothers
   c.   the need to create links with neighboring households by marrying a daughter to several different men
   d.   a belief that women have insatiable sexual appetites

28. Which of the following attributes was true of Nayar marriage practices until the end of the seventeenth century?
   a.   Husband and wife did not live together.
   b.   Women and men both had multiple spouses.
   c.   No attempt was made to determine the biological father of a woman's children.
* d.   All of the above are true.

29. Which of the following terms best describes traditional Inuit marriage?
   a.   wife-trading
   b.   polyandry
* c.   polygynandry
   d.   monogamy

30. Which of the following features distinguish Inuit marriage practices?
   a.   Women had no say about whether or not her husband took a second wife.
* b.   Divorce was impossible.
   c.   Having more than one spouse was impossible.
   d.   Marriages were alliance intensifying.

31. Among the Lovedu of southern Africa, the expression "cattle-linked siblings" refers to
   a.   sisters whose bridewealth came from the same herd of cattle.
   b.   brothers who will inherit cattle from the same herd.
* c.   the relationship that is created when a brother uses his sister's bridewealth cattle to get himself a wife.
   d.   the relationship that is created when a woman's brother gives cattle from his herd to her children on the occasion of their birth.

32. When a woman dies among the people of Mount Hagen, New Guinea, she is believed to continue to influence the fortunes of
  a.   her own clan, as a ghostly sister.
  b.   her husband's clan, as a ghostly mother.
  c.   nobody, since Hageners do not believe in ghosts.
* d.   both a and b

33. Which of the following observations about polygynous families is false?
  a.   Children with the same mother are not distinguished from children with different mothers.
  b.   Children of different wives are never jealous of one another since they learn to think of all the wives as "mothers" who are equally concerned about their welfare.
  c.   Disputes about inheritance are rare since only rich men capable of providing well for all his children can become polygynous in the first place.
* d.   All of the above are true.

34. Which of the following statements describes polygynous Mende households?
* a.   Wives are ranked by order of marriage.
  b.   Mende men and women agree that wives from high-status families outrank wives from lower-status families.
  c.   Serious problems arise if a husband shows favoritism toward a wife higher in the marriage ranking and neglects a wife from a high-status family.
  d.   Both b and c are true.

35. Which of the following statements describes the relationship of Mende women towards their children?
  a.   A Mende woman's children will inherit from her brother, and so she closely monitors how well her brother looks out for her children.
* b.   A Mende woman's principal claim to her husband's land or cash comes through her children.
  c.   Mende women have access to their own sources of wealth apart from husband and children.
  d.   Traditional Mende inheritance rules ordinarily leave widows well enough off to live comfortably on their own without depending on other kin.

36. Which of the following statements describes the attitude of Mende women towards the education of their children?

a. They favor informal instruction in traditional Mende customs to formal schooling.

* b. They care deeply about their children's formal education because better educated children earn more, and Mende women depend on their children to support them in old age.

c. They are more concerned to educate their daughters than their sons, because educated daughters bring in more bridewealth when they marry.

d. They believe that husbands should pay for their wives' education first, so the women can support themselves and pay for their children's education if the husband dies.

37. Families in which several generations live together in a single household are called

a. nuclear families.
* b. extended families.
c. joint families.
d. traditional families.

38. Families in which brothers and their wives (or sisters and their husbands) live together in a single household are called

a. nuclear families.
b. extended families.
* c. joint families.
d. traditional families.

39. According to Ivan Karp, Iteso women laugh during marriage rituals because

a. they are trying to disguise the fact that marriage is a hard lot for women.

b. they drink too much of the ritual beer.

c. their laughter is a ritual enactment of the autonomous position women enjoy in Iteso society once they have a husband.

* d. they recognize the irony in the fact that they, who are so closely controlled by men in marriage, nevertheless are in charge of the marriage ritual from which men are barred.

40. Comparative information on human sexual practices worldwide suggests that

a. the preservation of virginity until marriage is universally valued, especially for women.

b. a double standard, in which married men are free to take lovers but married women are not, is universally observed.

c. expectations of an active and satisfying sexual life is found everywhere.

* d. None of the above is true.

206

41. Ethnographic comparison has shown that
a.   forms of sexual expression unconnected to heterosexual reproduction are far from rare in human societies.
b.   several societies in New Guinea have instituted male homosexual practices as part of their initiation rituals.
c.   in Mombasa, Kenya, a marriage between a poor husband and a rich wife might be more shocking than a lesbian relationship between a dominant rich woman and a dependent poor one.
* d.   All of the above are true.

Essay Questions

42. What makes it possible for a Nuer woman to marry another woman and be the "father" of the children her wife bears? Discuss.

43. Why are the traditional marriage practices of the Nayar of India so important in any discussion of marriage and the family in cross-cultural perspective? Discuss.

44. Discuss what is meant by the expression "Cattle beget children."

45. Why do Iteso women laugh during marriage rituals? Discuss.

46. What are the similarities and differences between polygyny and polyandry? Discuss.

47. What are the four major rules for post-marital residence? What are some of the social, economic, and political consequences that follow from observance of each residence rule? Discuss.

48. What happens to Western sex role stereotypes when we pay close attention to relationships between sisters and brothers in different societies? Discuss.

49. Discuss the relationship of sex and marriage to power.

CHAPTER 20

BEYOND KINSHIP

Outline

KIN-BASED VERSUS NONKIN-BASED SOCIETIES

Status Versus Contract Relationships
Mechancal Versus Organic Solidarity
Ascribed Status and Achieved Status

METAPHORICAL KIN REVISITED

Friendship
Kinship in Nonkin Relationships

NONKIN TIES IN EGALITARIAN SOCIETIES: SODALITIES

Cheyenne Military Societies
Age Sets
Secret Societies in Western Africa

NONKIN TIES IN STRATIFIED SOCIETIES

Criteria for Membership in Levels of Society
Caste Societies
Class, Race, and Ethnicity

THE DIMENSIONS OF GROUP LIFE

Key Terms

status	achieved statuses	caste
role	sodalities	class
mechanical solidarity	age sets	race
organic solidarity	secret societies	ethnicity
division of labor	egalitarian soceties	clientage
ascribed statuses	stratified societies	

Arguing Anthropology

1. Why are nonkin social ties so important in places like the United States and Canada today?

2. Why is being "friendly" so important in student culture?

Multiple Choice Questions

1. Sir Henry Maine thought that kin-based societies differed from nonkin-based societies primarily because
   a. kin-based social relations were warm, supportive, and face-to-face, whereas life in a modern state required cold, anonymous interaction.
   b. societies based on kinship lacked the institutions of private property and the state, which characterized modern European society.
   * c. people in societies based on kinship were not free to choose their own statuses, nor could they modify the rights and responsibilities associated with those statuses, whereas citizens of modern European nation-states could do both.
   d. kin-based societies were held together by mechanical solidarity, whereas state societies were held together by organic solidarity.

2. Emile Durkheim thought that "primitive" societies differed from "modern" ones primarily because
   a. kin-based social relations were warm, supportive, and face-to-face, whereas life in a modern state required cold, anonymous interaction.
   b. societies based on kinship lacked the institutions of private property and the state, which characterized modern European society.
   c. people in societies based on kinship were not free to choose their own statuses, nor could they modify the rights and responsibilities associated with those statuses, whereas citizens of modern European nation-states could do both.
   * d. kin-based societies were held together by mechanical solidarity, whereas state societies were held together by organic solidarity.

3. Organic solidarity depends on
   a. face-to-face, multistranded social relations.
   b. a highly developed division of labor.
   c. the absence of private property.
   d. social organization based on status rather than contract.

4. Social statuses into which people are born are called
   a. achieved statuses.
   b. ascribed statuses.
   c. noble statuses.
   d. high statuses.

5. People may enter freely into relationships, and are equally free to specify the nature of the rights and obligations between them, in societies organized on the basis of
   a. status.
   b. role.
* c. contract.
   d. sodality.

6. Social statuses that people attain by their own efforts are called
* a. achieved statuses.
   b. ascribed statuses.
   c. noble statuses.
   d. high statuses.

7. "Daughter" and "son" are examples of
* a. ascribed statuses.
   b. achieved statuses.
   c. contractual statuses.
   d. innate statuses.

8. "Good hunter" or "good gatherer" are examples of
   a. ascribed statuses.
* b. achieved statuses.
   c. noble statuses.
   d. innate statuses.

9. For the Bangwa of Cameroon, the prototype of best friends are
* a. twins.
   b. brothers-in-law.
   c. sister and brother.
   d. joking relatives.

10. A key difference between friendship as it is understood in the United States and friendship among the Bangwa of Cameroon is that
* a. the Bangwa seal friendships with a ritual similar to that of marriage, and people in the United States do not.
   b. Bangwa friendships are short-term relationships whereas friendships in the United States typically last longer.
   c. Bangwa friendships are most intense among the young but diminish among older people, whereas in the United States just the opposite occurs.
   d. there are no key differences; the Bangwa think of friendship in the same way as people in the United States.

210

11. Anthropologist Michael Moffatt found that North American college students at Rutgers University in the 1980s
* a. thought that friends were the only freely chosen companions of equal status in their lives.
b. were unwilling to share "who they really were" with friends but would share this with close kin.
c. believed that everyone should act "friendly" only to their oldest, closest friends/
d. believed that there were obvious signs people could use to tell whether their friends were authentic or not.

12. Societies in which all members have equal access to wealth and power are called
a. bands.
b. tribes.
c. egalitarian societies.
d. all of the above

13. Societies in which some members have privileged access to prestige, but not to wealth or power are called
a. rank societies.
b. class societies.
c. caste societies.
d. band societies.

14. Societies with permanent hierarchies, in which some groups have privileged access to wealth, power, and prestige are called
a. rank societies.
b. stratified societies.
c. egalitarian societies.
d. none of the above

15. Stratified societies in which membership in each ranked group is closed and movement of individuals from one group to another is forbidden are called
a. rank societies.
b. caste societies.
c. class societies.
d. chiefdoms.

16. Stratified societies in which the members of internally ranked subgroups may pass out of one group into another are called
a. rank societies.
b. caste societies.
c. class societies.
d. chiefdoms.

17. According to Karl Marx, different social classes are determined by
* a.   the relationship of their members to the means of production.
   b.   occupational specialization.
   c.   race and ethnicity.
   d.   all of the above

18. In addition to India, caste systems can be found in
   a.   Tierra del Fuego.
* b.   Sudanic West Africa.
   c.   Highland New Guinea.
   d.   Madagascar.

19. The Oruro Devil Fraternity, a Bolivian organization devoted to the Virgin of Socavon, is an example of
* a.   a sodality.
   b.   an age set.
   c.   a secret society.
   d.   none of the above

20. Special-purpose groupings that may be organized on the basis of age, sex, economic role, or personal interest are called
   a.   statuses.
* b.   sodalities.
   c.   classes.
   d.   castes.

21. In the United States, which of the following are similar to age set systems?
   a.   church youth groups
   b.   New York Yankees fans
   c.   all of the cousins in your family
* d.   the group of children who entered kindergarten together

22. Garrison Keillor says Lake Wobegon is a socialist society rather than a free enterprise society because
   a.   the residents are very social people.
   b.   the residents are all committed communists.
* c.   the community runs on loyalty rather than self-interest.
   d.   the residents have socialized medicine.

23. Which of the following nonkin forms of social organization has been described as an "unsuccessful attempt to tame time by chopping it up into manageable slices"?
   a.   Cheyenne military societies
* b.   East African age sets
   c.   western African secret societies
   d.   none of the above

24. In eastern African age set systems, married men cannot prevent sexual relationships that might develop between their wives and their age-mates because
   a.   eastern Africans practice group marriage.
* b.   age mates are forbidden to take offense at anything they say or do to each other.
   c.   unmarried men have higher status than married men.
   d.   women in these societies enjoy unusual sexual autonomy.

25. Which of the following features allows age mates in Nyakusa society to enjoy ukwangala?
   a.   building in villages rather than in scattered homesteads
   b.   fathers and sons sharing food and beer with one another
   c.   living close to one's kin
   d.   both b and c

26. According to P.T.W. Baxter, the age set system of the Boran of Kenya is best understood as
   a.   a form of political organization.
   b.   a way of preventing incest between a man's father and his wife.
   c.   a means of ensuring the well-being of society and regulating the ritual growth of individuals.
   d.   a way of providing an outlet for youthful high spirits while simultaneously protecting Boran society from enemies.

27. Among peoples like the Mende, Kpelle, and Sherbro, membership in a secret society is attained by
   a.   paying a fee.
   b.   undergoing initiation.
   c.   being born into the right lineage.
   d.   having relatives on your mother's side of the family who belong.

28. The secrecy in the secret societies of western Africa concerns
   a.   who the members are.
   b.   knowing when, how, and whether to speak about various topics.
   c.   who is dancing inside the masks representing the supernaturals.
 * d.   both b and c

29. Carol MacCormack describes the Thoma secret society of the Sherbro as a microcosm because
   a.   very few people are allowed to become members.
   b.   its members also belong to Poro and Sande congregations.
 * c.   both men and women belong.
   d.   both adults and children belong.

30. According to Beryl Bellman and his Kpelle informants, women speak of devils killing and eating Poro initiates because
   a.   they believe this to be literally true.
   b.   they are not allowed to talk about the intiation except in the language of ritual metaphor.
   c.   the "audience" of women and other noninitiates plays an important ritual role in Poro initiation.
 * d.   both b and c are true

31. A set of prototypically descent-based cultural criteria that people in a group are believed to share is referred to as
   a.   caste.
   b.   class.
   c.   race.
 * d.   ethnicity.

32. When individuals belonging to upper and lower levels in a stratified society are linked socially, anthropologists call their relationship
   a.   false consciousness.
 * b.   clientage.
   c.   patronage.
   d.   caste.

33. The residents of Gopalpur believe that members of each jati
   a.   are related by ties of kinship.
   b.   marry only among themselves.
   c.   follow particular practices and occupations.
 * d.   all of the above

34. In the Hindu ranking of jatis in terms of purity and pollution, which of the following activities is the least polluting?
* a. a vegetarian diet
 b. eating sheep and goats
 c. butchering animals
 d. washing dirty clothing

35. When people in Gopalpur say that members of different jatis should not "eat together," they actually mean that
 a. all the jatis never participate together in any public rituals that involve food consumption.
* b. members of different jatis should not eat from the same dish or sitting on the same line.
 c. members of jatis that are close in rank and neither at the top nor at the bottom of the scale should not eat together.
 d. jatis may not eat together unless they are eating rice.

36. The economic status of any particular jati in Gopalpur
 a. is the same as the status of that jati on the scale of purity and pollution.
* b. has no direct correlation with the status of that jati on the scale of purity and pollution.
 c. depends on its ties to local Brahmins
 d. is unusual in India, in that all jatis are prosperous and remarkably independent of the influence of local landlords.

37. In Gopalpur, the interdependence of different jatis is most important in which context?
 a. ritual
 b. everyday
 c. economic
 d. leisure

38. Marghi blacksmiths are regarded by other Marghi with
 a. contempt.
 b. awe.
 c. derision.
 d. hatred.

39. Whether the Spanish word casta should be translated "caste" or "class" or "race" or "ethnic group" is an interesting question because
a.   the original "estates" whose interbreeding produced the castas were defined in terms of race.
b.   since Spaniards monopolized wealth, power, and prestige in Mexico, they could be viewed as the ruling class, with everyone else making up the subject class.
c.   members of the original colonial estates differed from one another in culture, so they might be seen as constituting separate ethnic groups.
* d.   All of the above are true.

40. Some mestizos and mulattoes in colonial Oaxaca were allowed to carry arms, an elite privilege. This suggests to John Chance that
a.   the sistema de castas actually had no effect on upward mobility in the colony.
b.   Concern with indigenous ancestry and African ancestry disappeared in Oaxaca as soon as there were enough mestizos and mulattoes to attract attention.
* c.   the status of mestizos and mulattoes was ambiguous in colonial Oaxaca.
d.   Both a and b are true.

Essay Questions

41. Discuss the different ways early anthropologists and sociologists attempted to explain the shift from kin-based society to nonkin-based society.

42. What are the similarities and differences between caste in India and caste among the Marghi of West Africa?

43. What social functions can be performed by sodalities that kinship groups cannot perform? Discuss and give examples.

44. Discuss the role of secrecy in Kpelle society.

45. What does Garrison Keillor mean when he says that if people in Lake Wobegon were to live by comparison shopping, the town would go bust? Discuss.

46. In what ways may friendship be considered a kind of metaphorical kinship? Discuss.

47. What is "diffuse and enduring solidarity"? How is it generated in human society?

48. Describe the operation of the sistema de castas in colonial Oaxaca. What does the history of this system of social organization tell us about social categories in human societies?

CHAPTER 21

SOCIAL ORGANIZATION AND POWER

Outline

Key Terms

social organization
power
political anthropology
coercion
legitimacy

autonomy
consensus
persuasion
anomie

alienation
negotiation
essentially negotiable
   concepts

Arguing Anthropology

1. When students feel powerless in a university environment, do they employ strategies similar to the ones discussed in the two text sections, The Power of the Weak and Negotiation?

2. How will nations decide to support one faction rather than another in international trouble spots, when the old lessons fo history that saw the world in terms of superpower rivalry no longer seem to apply?

Multiple Choice Questions

1. Unilineal evolutionists in the nineteenth century believed that the inflexible laws of social organization were rooted in
* a.   history.
  b.   the local environment in which a society was embedded.
  c.   cultural borrowing.
  d.   genetic programming.

2. The patterning of human interdependence in a given society through the actions and decisions of its members is called
  a.   hierarchy.
  b.   equality.
* c.   social organization.
  d.   economy.

3. Perhaps the most important and controversial contribution of anthropology to the debate about laws of social organization is the argument that
* a.   there is no way to reduce the complexities of human societies to a single underlying cause.
  b.   genes determine culture.
  c.   environment determines culture.
  d.   culture can be explained by the laws of history.

4. Anthropologist I. M. Lewis compared the social organization of the northern Somalis and the Boran Galla, who live next to each other in semiarid scrubland and herd the same animals. His comparison showed that
  a.   environment determines social structure.
* b.   the Somali and the Boran are quite different in social structure.
  c.   the Somali and the Boran are virtually identical in social structure.
  d.   Both a and c are true.

5. According to anthropologist Marshall Sahlins, the response of any given society to population pressure
   a. will be identical.
* b. can be varied.
   c. always results in the development of new forms of birth control.
   d. both a and c

6. Which of the following terms is used by Eric Wolf to refer to the form of social power that organizes social settings and controls the allocation of social labor?
   a. interpersonal power
   b. organizational power
* c. structural power
   d. legitimate power

7. Which of the following is a topic of interest to political anthropologists?
   a. the classification and evolution of political systems
   b. the structure and functions of political systems
   c. the modernization of formerly tribal societies
* d all of the above

8. In traditional Western thought, the prototype of power in human social relations is based on
   a. physical coercion.
   b. negotiation.
   c. ability to convince.
   d. all of the above

9. Research by political anthropologists has led to a reconsideration of
   a. the political role of the state.
   b. the political role of kinship.
   c. traditional Western notions about human nature.
   d. all of the above

10. Power based on force is called
   a. legitimacy.
   b. coercion.
   c. autonomy.
   d. persuasion.

11. Power based on group consensus is called
* a.   legitimacy.
  b.   coercion.
  c.   motivation.
  d.   persuasion.

12. According to Evans-Pritchard, the Azande attitude towards witchcraft was
  a.   one of constant fear.
* b.   more likely to be anger than fear.
  c.   one of helplessness, since their belief system offered no way of coping with witchcraft.
  d.   irrational.

13. According to Alma Gottlieb, in order for a Beng king to be considered legitimate,
  a.   he must be able to show that he is untainted by association with witchcraft.
* b.   he must use witchcraft to kill three close matrinlineal relatives within his first year of rule.
  c.   he must renounce witchcraft in order to show his independence from control by his own kinship group.
  d.   he must show that he operates on the same plane of common morality as those over whom he rules.

14. An approach to the study of social organization that describes political engagement as a form of haggling
  a.   views the parties to political negotiation as free agents.
  b.   assumes that individuals are not and should not be influenced by obligations to other that deter them from following their individual self-interest.
  c.   assumes that individuals in society are bound by collective obligations for each other's welfare.
* d.   both a and b

15. In the stateless societies of native North and South America, power is understood to be
* a.   independent of human beings.
  b.   a negotiated relationship between people with different resources.
  c.   derived from the consent of the governed.
  d.   physical coercion.

16. Which of the following statements is a consequence of assuming that power is part of the natural order of things yet is independent of direct human control?
    a.   Power and violence go hand in hand.
*   b.   Power and violence are antithetical.
    c.   Power lies in the human imagination.
    d.   All of the above are true.

17. If people see power as an entity external to themselves, the only power individuals possess is
    a.   puny and unimportant.
    b.   that which they accumulate for themselves through great deeds of valor.
*   c.   the right not to be forced by violence to do the will of others.
    d.   none of the above

18. When application of physical force is recognized as a cure worse than the political ills it seeks to remove, there is no alternative but
    a.   nuclear war.
    b.   metaphorical competition, as in the form of the Olympic Games.
*   c.   negotiation.
    d.   surrender.

19. Moroccan men and women live
    a.   ambilocally.
    b.   matrilocally.
    c.   neolocally.
*   d.   side by side in different worlds.

20. Which of the following figures described social life without the state as a "war of all against all"?
    a.   E. E. Evans-Pritchard
    b.   Ted Lewellen
*   c.   Thomas Hobbes
    d.   Lewis Henry Morgan

21. The assertion that the application of enough naked force can make anybody submit to any social system has a difficult time accounting for the existence of
    a.   witchcraft beliefs.
    b.   religion.
    c.   martyrs.
    d.   electoral politics.

22. According to Pierre Clastres, the most respected members of stateless societies are
   a.   initiated men.
* b.   persuasive speakers.
   c.   men or women who have been able to amass coercive power.
   d.   old people.

23. The power to resist the imposition of other people's choices is the power of
   a.   a free agent.
   b.   a rational human being.
* c.   an autonomous individual.
   d.   fantasy.

24. Which of the following terms was used by Emile Durkheim to describe the sense of normlessless and rootlessness experienced by many members of his society?
* a.   anomie
   b.   alienation
   c.   anonymity
   d.   mechanical solidarity

25. Which of the following terms was used by Karl Marx to describe the deep separation workers seemed to experience between their innermost sense of identity and the labor they were forced to perform to earn enough money to live?
   a.   anomie
* b.   alienation
   c.   anonymity
   d.   mechanical solidarity

26. According to Hoyt Alverson, most Tswana migrants whom he interviewed
   a.   were alienated and dehumanized.
   b.   lacked any means of coping with the oppression they had suffered in the gold mines of South Africa.
* c.   led coherent and meaningful lives despite their involvement in an exploitative system.
   d.   both a and b

27. The traditional folktale character in many societies who lives by his wits is basically amoral and is happy to hoodwink anyone who tries to take advantage of him is known as
   a.　　Tio.
   b.　　Ch'alla.
 * c.　　Trickster.
   d.　　Sedaka.

28. Older Tswana migrants who recounted their life histories to Hoyt Alverson
   a.　　were classic illustrations of the "scars of bondage" thesis.
 * b.　　saw themselves as Tricksters.
   c.　　described how they had turned the Ch'alla ritual against the mine owners.
   d.　　described how they had eventually given up their devotion to Tswana traditions

29. According to James Scott, occasional arrests, warnings, legal restrictions, and indefinite preventive detention are examples of
   a.　　everyday forms of peasant resistance.
   b.　　unusual forms of peasant resistance.
   c.　　unusual forms of repression.
 * d.　　routine repression.

30. According to James Scott, foot dragging, desertion, pilfering, slander, arson, and sabotage are examples of
 * a.　　everyday forms of peasant resistance.
   b.　　unusual forms of peasant resistance.
   c.　　unusual forms of repression.
   d.　　routine repression.

31. In Sedaka, rich and poor villagers alike agreed that
   a.　　the benefits of combine harvesters outweigh their costs.
   b.　　the costs of combine harvesters outweigh their benefits.
 * c.　　using combine harvesters hurts the poor and helps the rich.
   d.　　using combine harvesters helps the poor and hurts the rich.

32. Before the Bolivian tin mines were nationalized, the ch'alla ritual embodied
   a.　　conflict between mine owners and mine workers.
 * b.　　harmonious ties between mine owners and mine workers.
   c.　　conflict between male miners and female miners.
   d.　　cooperation between male miners and female miners.

33. According to Scott, the struggle between rich and poor villagers in Sedaka
  a. was a struggle over work and property rights.
  b. was a struggle over how the past and present shall be understood and labeled.
  c. was a struggle over the appropriation of symbols.
* d. all of the above

34. In the example of a Moroccan marriage negotiation related by Lawrence Rosen, the young girl eventually married the young man her father had chosen because
  a. she was persuaded that it was her duty to submit to her father's will.
  b. the young man chosen for her agreed to move to Sefrou.
* c. she was persuaded that the marriage made good economic sense.
  d. her mother sided with her father.

35. The marriage negotiation described by Rosen in Sefrou, Morocco shows how
  a. women may agree with the male position in general terms and yet dispute its relevance in a particular situation.
  b. men may get women to comply with their wishes, and yet women's reasons for doing so may have nothing to do with the reasons men offer to justify their demands.
  c. women and men share the same moral perspective and interpreted the young girl's resistance to her proposed marriage in the same way, despite the very separate worlds in which Moroccan women and men live.
* d. Both a and b are true.

36. Beginning in the 1970s, the rondas campesinas of northern Peru developed as
  a. the first soldiers of the Maoist Shining Path movement.
* b. new rural justice groups designed to combat animal rustlers.
  c. new folkloric dance groups responding to increased tourism in the area.
  d. groups of peasants taking advantage of the opportunities provided by land reform.

37. During the 1980s, the scope of the rondas campesinas
* a. expanded into an entire alternative justice system with open peasant assemblies to resolve a wide range of disputes.
  b. contracted as a result of increased government involvement in northern Peru.
  c. contracted as a result of increasing corruption among ronda leaders.
  d. spread to southern Peru and led to the creation of a national dance troupe that represented Peru in international competitions.

38. Which of the following statements describes the relationship between the rondas campesinas and the rest of Peruvian culture?
a.   Ronda organization was completely new and owed nothing to the rest of Peruvian culture.
* b.   The rondas see themselves as genuine upholders of the law and the Peruvian constitution.
c.   The rondas made a decisive break from Peruvian tradition by permitting women to hold powerful positions as ronda leaders.
d.   Both b and c are true.

39. According to Orin Starn, over time the rondas campesinas have
a.   grown more violent.
b.   let peasants down by turning into arms of the traditional justice system.
* c.   given Peruvian peasants the vision of an alternative modernity.
d.   corrupted indigenous traditions in order to become more commercially viable.

40. To say that the central symbols of any cultural tradition are essentially negotiable means that
a.   symbols can mean anything an individual wants them to mean.
* b.   each symbol evokes a wide range of meanings among those who accept it.
c.   what each symbol means in any particular context is obvious to members of the culture.
d.   the people with the greatest coercive power will always manage to make their account triumph over alternatives.

Essay Questions

41. Discuss the way power is understood in state and stateless societies.

42. Power as a form of individual autonomy is notoriously difficult to erase from human consciousness, often to the frustration of political leaders. How does Alverson's discussion of the Tswana illustrate this?

43. Anthropologist Richard N. Adams has said, "It is useful to accept the proposition that, while men have in some sense always been equal (i.e. in that each always has some independent power), they have in another sense never been equal." Discuss, with examples.

44. The "scars of bondage" thesis argues that the more complete the political domination and exploitation of a people, the more deeply they will be scarred by the experience. Discuss, with examples.

45. Alverson discusses the figure of the Trickster in Tswana folklore. Describe trickster characters in American folklore. Might they serve as prototypes for survival in our own society? Discuss.

46. Are the forms of "everyday peasant resistance" described by Scott found only in peasant societies? Can you think of examples of behavior in American society that could be described in similar terms? What might this suggest about the circumstances in which practitioners of these actions live? Discuss.

47. How is power based on persuasion possible?

48. What is a "Big Man" or a man with influence? What kinds of power does he have? From where does he get his power?

49. "Politics is . . . very much a matter of struggling over meaning, not just of physical coercion." Discuss, using examples.

CHAPTER 22

MAKING A LIVING

Outline

CULTURE AND LIVELIHOOD

SUBSISTENCE STRATEGIES

DISTRIBUTION, PRODUCTION, AND CONSUMPTION

Distribution and Exchange Theory
Production Theory
Concumption Theory

A DIALECTIC BETWEEN THE MEANINGFUL AND THE MATERIAL

Key Terms

scarcity	consumption	market exchange
economy	exchange	labor
subsistence strategies	neoclassical economic	mode of production
food collectors	theory	means of production
food producers	formalists	relations of production
extensive agriculture	rational	ideology
intensive agriculture	substantivists	ecology
mechanized industrial	modes of exchange	niche
agriculture	reciprocity	ecozone
production	redistribution	affluence
distribution		

Arguing Anthropology

1. From an anthropological perspective, why don't North Americans eat dogs?

2. In light of the discussion in this chapter, what might the famous phrase "You are what you eat" mean?

Multiple Choice Questions

1. The assumption that people's resources will never be great enough for them to obtain all the goods they desire is called

* a.   scarcity.
  b.   poverty.
  c.   utility.
  d.   affluence.

2. For more than 90 percent of human history, our ancestors lived by
   a. cultivation.
   b. herding.
 * c. foraging.
   d. intensive agriculture.

3. Which of the following is a definition of "economy" that has been used by anthropologists?
   a. maximizing utility
   b. an institutional process of interaction which functions to provide material means in society
   c. obtaining as much satisfaction as possible for the smallest possible cost
 * d. all of the above

4. The agricultural technique in which a plot of land is burned, cultivated, and then allowed to lie fallow for several years is called
   a. intensive agriculture.
 * b. extensive agriculture.
   c. industrial agriculture.
   d. mechanized agriculture.

5. Which of the following describes the way European feudal societies handled distribution?
 * a. Goods and services were allotted to different social groups and individuals on the basis of status.
   b. Goods and services were allocated to different individuals on the basis of supply and demand.
   c. Every individual family produced and consumed its own goods and services, thus making distribution unnecessary.
   d. None of the above are true.

6. Neoclassical economic theory is based on which of the following assumptions?
   a. The market determines production and consumption levels.
   b. scarcity
   c. People are rational.
 * d. all of the above

7. Capitalist economic relations were considered "free" because
   a. consumer goods were more readily available.
   b. demand for basic subsistence goods was decreased.
* c. ascribed social status no longer determined a person's access to goods.
   d. prices for goods were so low, compared to prices under feudalism, that all people could spend next to nothing and still satisfy all their consumption needs.

8. Substantivists suggest that capitalist market exchange is but
   a. one mode of production.
   b. one mode of consumption.
* c. one mode of exchange.
   d. one mode of discourse.

9. Formalist economic anthropologists did not view their approach to nonWestern economies as ethnocentric because
   a. they believed that their theory was scientific and universal.
   b. they believed nonWestern people were as rational as they were.
   c. they believed all human beings operate out of self-interest.
* d. All of the above are true.

10. Substantivist Karl Polanyi suggested three modes of exchange that could be identified historically and cross-culturally. These are
* a. reciprocity, redistribution, market exchange.
   b. production, consumption, redistribution.
   c. barter, cash exchange, credit.
   d. trade, money, and market.

11. Which of the following is an example of redistribution?
   a. potlatch
   b. Internal Revenue Service
   c. Salvation Army
* d. all of the above

12. The most ancient mode of exchange was
   a. redistribution.
* b. reciprocity.
   c. market.
   d. money.

13. Contemporary economic anthropologists, according to Stuart Plattner, accept which of the following propositions?
* a.   economies are embedded in other cultural institutions
   b.   the economic choices of nonWestern peoples are governed by the maximizing "rationality" of capitalism
   c.   "economizing" behavior exists everywhere
   d.   scarcity is the creation of capitalist social relations

14. The capitalist mode of production is characterized by
   a.   private ownership of the means of production.
   b.   the selling of labor power on the market.
   c.   the generation of surplus wealth.
* d.   all of the above

15. For Marx, the activity linking human social groups to the material world around them was
   a.   scarcity.
   b.   exchange.
* c.   labor.
   d.   class.

16. Each mode of production suggests
   a.   what a society's subsistence strategy is.
   b.   how people organize themselves to carry out the subsistence strategy they employ.
   c.   lines of cleavage in the society along which tension and conflict may develop.
* d.   all of the above

17. In order to find enough food to survive, Richard Lee suggests that foraging peoples like the Ju/'hoansi (!Kung) must work
   a.   almost constantly.
   b.   about 40-50 hours per week per person.
   c.   about three hours per week per person.
* d.   under 20 hours per week per person.

18. Marshall Sahlins coined the expression "the original affluent society" to describe
* a.   the Ju/'hoansi (!Kung) and others like them.
   b.   Europeans in the nineteenth century.
   c.   Americans in the twentieth century.
   d.   Chinese in the fourteenth century.

19. According to Marshall Sahlins, which of the following is a route to affluence?
   a.   colonial conquest
   b.   producing much
   c.   desiring little
 * d.   both b and c

20. An anthropological attempt to apply the insights of ecology to human beings and their societies is called
   a.   economic anthropology.
 * b.   cultural ecology.
   c.   production theory.
   d.   exchange theory.

21. To be rational in terms of neoclassical economic theory means
   a.   to think and act in accord with the central principles of one's culture.
 * b.   to be concerned first and foremost with one's individual self-interest.
   c.   to accept the principles of syllogistic reasoning.
   d.   to go beyond the information given.

22. The theft of your CD player by housebreakers would be an example of which mode of exchange?
   a.   generalized reciprocity
   b.   balanced reciprocity
 * c.   negative reciprocity
   d.   redistribution

23. In the societies of early modern Europe, trade, money, and markets came together to create
   a.   balanced reciprocity.
   b.   negative reciprocity.
   c.   redistribution.
 * d.   market exchange.

24. From the perspective of production theory, the tools, skills, organization, and knowledge used to extract energy from nature are called
   a.   the mode of production.
 * b.   the means of production.
   c.   the relations of production.
   d.   labor.

25. Products of consciousness, such as morality, religion, and metaphysics that purport to explain to people who they are and to justify to them the kind of lives they lead are called
   a.　　social labor.
   b.　　modes of production.
 * c.　　ideology.
   d.　　relations of production.

26. Which of the following has been highlighted by an emphasis on production theory in economic anthropology?
   a.　　the way access to resources is determined before exchange takes place
   b.　　the way the relations of production shape the way people choose to buy and sell
   c.　　the way human beings are viewed as social agents involved in the construction and reconstruction of human society on all levels in every generation
 * d.　　all of the above

27. According to Marx, the potential for social conflict is
   a.　　rare in human societies, which naturally tend toward harmony.
   b.　　only found in the capitalist mode of production.
 * c.　　built into every mode of production.
   d.　　irrational.

28. The using up of material goods necessary for human physical survival is called
   a.　　production.
   b.　　distribution.
   c.　　exchange.
 * d.　　consumption.

29. To the question, "Why do people X raise peanuts and sorghum?", Malinowski would reply
 * a.　　to meet their basic human need for food
   b.　　because peanuts and sorghum are the only food crops available in their ecozone that, when cultivated, will meet their subsistence needs
   c.　　because to eat peanuts and sorghum is simultaneously to make an important statement of social identity in society X
   d.　　because both foods taken together provide complete proteins

30. Which of the following answers would a cultural ecologist be most likely to provide for the question, "Why do people X raise peanuts and sorghum?"
   - a.   to meet their basic human need for food
   - * b.   because peanuts and sorghum are the only food crops available in their ecozone that, when cultivated, will meet their subsistence needs
   - c.   because to eat peanuts and sorghum is simultaneously to make an important statement of social identity in society X
   - d.   because both foods taken together provide complete proteins

31. Anthropologists have always held that every society must understand its local ecology because
   - a.   each society can only consume its own local resources.
   - b.   patterns of consumption are dictated by an iron environmental necessity that does not allow alternatives.
   - c.   societies will die out unless they consume every edible resource that is locally available.
   - * d.   the way a society chooses to make use of its resources can have serious consequences for its own survival and the survival of future generations.

32. According to Mary Douglas and Baron Isherwood, the distinction between "necessities" and "luxuries"
   - a.   is fundamental to any sound analysis of consumption patterns.
   - * b.   is not helpful and should be ignored in the analysis of consumption patterns.
   - c.   distinguishes the subject matter of production studies from the subject matter of consumption studies.
   - d.   is helpful only when analyzing consumption patterns in capitalist societies.

33. According to Mary Douglas, the Jewish prohibition against eating pork
   - a.   is meaningless and irrational.
   - * b.   makes sense when placed in the context of other Jewish dietary prohibitions.
   - c.   is paralleled in many other societies living in ecological settings similar to that of the ancient Hebrews.
   - d.   is based on a scientific understanding of the health risks associated with pork in societies without antibiotics or refrigeration.

34. Among the Trobriand Islanders, women's wealth
   - a.   is insignificant.
   - * b.   is exchanged for yams.
   - c.   was first described by Bronislaw Malinowski.
   - d.   both a and c

35. According to Annette Weiner, the exchange of banana leaf bundles during mortuary rituals in the Trobriands
   a.   is a classic example of irrational consumption.
   b.   has become more important as a result of Western influence on traditional Trobriand culture.
* c.   allows Trobrianders to represent and affirm the most fundamental relationships in their social system.
   d.   has been dominated by men in recent years.

36. Annette Weiner argues that the role of women's wealth in Trobriand society
   a.   had increased since Malinowski first visited the field.
   b.   was less important today than it was when Malinowski first described it in 1917.
* c.   could disappear if cash ever became widely substitutable for yams.
   d.   had been substantially undermined by colonial rule.

37. The economic arrangements of the Plains Cree are an example of what happens when
   a.   the individual desire for self-betterment is thwarted.
   b.   greed becomes institutionalized.
* c.   sharing becomes institutionalized.
   d.   negative reciprocity is institutionalized.

38. According to Braroe, the rule about sharing among the Plains Cree seemed to be
   a.   goods only must be shared on public occasions, like giveaway dances.
* b.   any visible resource may legitimately be requested by another.
   c.   only band leaders who have become wealthy are expected to show spontaneous generosity.
   d.   consumption goods should be shared with other lineage members and not throughout the band as a whole.

39. Anthropologist Nick Fiddes argues that
   a.   the North American classification of animals as livestock or pets maximizes efficiency and minimizes waste.
   b.   eating organ meats is is a form of metaphorical cannibalism.
   c.   human beings are by nature carnivores.
* d.   meat's high status in Western societies is due to the fact that it represents human control of the natural world.

40. Marshall Sahlins argues that
a.   beef tongue has superior nutritional value, which is reflected in its high price.
* b.   North Americans do not approve of eating meat that comes from animals that have been treated as members of the family.
c.   the distinction which Americans make between livestock and pets is found in all human societies.
d.   the classification of cattle, pigs, horses, and dogs as edible or inedible is based on a rational understanding of their respective nutritional value.

Essay Questions

41. Describe the different modes of exchange operating in the society of the United States. What are their interrelationships with one another? Give examples.

42. What is meant by the claim that consumption needs are culturally shaped? Discuss and illustrate with examples.

43. Dietary prohibitions become intelligible when they are not taken individually but reembedded in the cultural pattern from which they came. Discuss with reference to the prohibition of pork consumption among Jews and Muslims.

44. Do Americans have food taboos? Discuss, and give examples.

45. "Goods assembled in ownership make physical, visible statements about the hierarchy of values to which their chooser subscribes." Discuss and give examples.

46. Describe and discuss the three major modes of exchange recognized by anthropologists, giving examples of each.

47. What is a mode of production? Describe and discuss the three major modes of production outlined by Eric Wolf.

48. What are the advantages and disadvantages for economic anthropologists who choose to emphasize either distribution, production, or consumption in their analyses?

49. "A dialectic between the meaningful and the material is the underlying basis for the modes of livelihood followed by human beings everywhere." Discuss.

CHAPTER 23

THE WORLD SYSTEM

Outline

THE GROWTH OF WESTERN CAPITALISM AND WESTERN
EXPANSION

The Colonial Political Economy
The Key Metaphor of Capitalism
Accounting for Social and Cultural Change
The Roots of the Neocolonial Order
Women and Colonization

VIEWS OF THE POLITICAL ECONOMY

Modernization Theory
Dependency Theory
World-System Theory
Neomarxian Theory
Current Trends

MODES OF CHANGE IN THE MODERN WORLD

The Power of Persuasion
The Power of the Gun

Arguing Anthropology

1. Why should anyone care about the world's indigenous peoples?

2. What is the justification for Christian missionary activity in the non-
   Christian world, from the point of view of (1) missionaries; (2) the
   governments of the nations in which the missionaries work; (3) local people
   being missionized; (4) anthropologists; (5) you yourself?

Multiple Choice Questions

1. Creating a reserve for the Kréen-Akaróre had what effect?
* a.   The Kréen-Akaróre abandoned their gardens and aborted their babies
  b.   Their population increased and, eventually, they required more land.
  c.   They became employed by establishments along the new highway.
  d.   Many of them became eloquent spokespeople for environmental and
          other advocacy groups whose goal was protection of the Amazon Rain
          Forest.

2. Political conquest of one society by another, followed by cultural domination with enforced social change, is a definition of
   a. capitalism.
 * b. colonialism.
   c. feudalism.
   d. ethnocentrism.

3. The key metaphor of capitalism is
 * a. the world is a market and everything has its price.
   b. those whose live by the sword die by the sword.
   c. the word for the world is forest.
   d. nature takes care of her children.

4. A significant transformation in the nonWestern world that resulted from contact with Western capitalism has been
   a. a dramatic improvement in the standard of living for the majority of the nonWestern world's people.
 * b. the growth of cities.
   c. an increasing respect for the environment.
   d. stronger protection of the rights of indigenous peoples.

5. In small-scale nonWestern societies without states, land traditionally
   a. could be bought and sold only among relatives.
   b. was the possession of the most powerful people.
 * c. was the possession of the social group that used it.
   d. could be bought and sold on the open market.

6. Complex commercial activity
   a. was invented by Western capitalism.
   b. was borrowed from Europe by Chinese and Indian entrepreneurs who used it to develop the first sophisticated economic systems ever seen in their societies.
 * c. was developed in parts of the world like China and India before the spread of capitalism, and prepared elites in those lands to take advantage of the new opportunities capitalism offered.
   d. cannot exist unless people are willing to turn anything and everything into commodities that can be sold on the market.

7. In order to operate mines in South Africa at a profit, the British
   a. imposed taxes that could only be paid in cash.
   b. prevented the development of a cash economy in traditional African areas.
   c. eliminated African self-sufficiency.
 * d. all of the above

8. The example of the Kayapo in Brazil demonstrates that
   a.   indigenous peoples are helpless "victims of progress."
 * b.   indigenous peoples can ally themselves with one another to defend environmental, human, and tribal rights.
   c.   sacred persuasion works.
   d.   secular persuasion works.

9. A holistic term that attempts to capture the centrality of material interest and the use of power to defend that interest is
 * a.   political economy.
   b.   sacred persuasion.
   c.   secular persuasion.
   d.   articulating modes of production.

10. Independence was granted to most European colonies
   a.   before World War II.
 * b.   after World War II.
   c.   in the nineteenth century.
   d.   after World War I.

11. American anthropologists in the 1930s
 * a.   believed it was possible to study social and cultural change in an impartial and scientific manner.
   b.   advocated particular political positions to encourage change.
   c.   were active in promoting schemes for economic development.
   d.   none of the above

12. Political independence for colonies
   a.   led to a return to traditional ways.
 * b.   made little economic difference.
   c.   allowed the citizens of new states to take complete control of their own economic destinies.
   d.   both a and c

13. Continued economic and political influence by former colonial powers following the political independence of their former colonies is called
   a.   capitalism
   b.   colonialism
 * c.   neocolonialism
   d.   neoconservatism

238

14. Weaving among the Baule of the Ivory Coast was traditionally done by
 a.   women.
* b.   men.
 c.   unmarried girls.
 d.   postmenopausal women.

15. For the Baule of the Ivory Coast, raising cotton and spinning thread was traditionally done by
* a.   women.
 b.   men.
 c.   their neighbors the Beng.
 d.   both a and c

16. When the Ivory Coast became a colony of France the traditional order of the Baule was upset because
 a.   factory-spun thread was sold for cash.
 b.   men were made responsible for paying their wives' taxes in cash.
 c.   men were taught how to grow cash crop cotton.
* d.   All of the above are true.

17. As a result of cash-cropping and the presence of the textile factory in Baule country,
 a.   Baule women lost status and power in their marriages.
 b.   many Baule women choose not to marry.
 c.   many Baule women prefer to acquire their own cash through wage labor.
* d.   All of the above are true.

18. Which of the following is an assumption of Dependency Theory?
 a.   Young states, like young men, develop according to an innate timetable.
* b.   Western prosperity relied on the exploitation of materials and markets that colonies provided.
 c.   When European capitalism expanded beyond its borders, beginning in the late fifteenth and early sixteenth centuries, it incorporated other regions and peoples into a world economy that was not an empire.
 d.   Third World countries are best understood as a series of social formations characterized by articulating modes of production.

19. Modernization theory assumes which of the following?
* a.   Young states, like young men, develop according to an innate timetable.
   b.   Western prosperity relied on the exploitation of materials and markets that colonies provided.
   c.   When European capitalism expanded beyond its borders beginning in the late fifteenth and early sixteenth centuries, it incorporated other regions and peoples into a world economy that was not an empire.
   d.   Third World countries are best understood as a series of social formations characterized by articulating modes of production.

20. World-system theory assumes which of the following?
   a.   Young states, like young men, develop according to an innate timetable.
   b.   Western prosperity relied on the exploitation of materials and markets that colonies provided.
* c.   When European capitalism expanded beyond its borders, beginning in the late fifteenth and early sixteenth centuries, it incorporated other regions and peoples into a world economy that was not an empire.
   d.   Third World countries are best understood as a series of social formations characterized by articulating modes of production.

21. Which of the following statements is characteristic of neomarxian theory?
   a.   Young states, like young men, develop according to an innate timetable.
   b.   Western prosperity relied on the exploitation of materials and markets that colonies provided.
   c.   When European capitalism expanded beyond its borders, beginning in the late fifteenth and early sixteenth centuries, it incorporated other regions and peoples into a world economy that was not an empire.
* d.   Third World countries are best understood as a series of social formations characterized by articulating modes of production.

22. The core of the world economy consists of nations specializing in
* a.   banking, finance, and highly skilled industrial production.
   b.   agriculture, pastoralism, and food production.
   c.   unskilled industrial production.
   d.   mining of gems and precious metals.

23. Immanuel Wallerstein argues that
a.   modern nation-states can develop only if they follow the model of the United States and Western Europe.
* b.   the notion that modern nation-states are independent entities engaged in balanced exchange in a free market is false.
c.   the same dependency relationships that link an underdeveloped country to a developed country are found in the underdeveloped country itself, down to the level of the smallest village.
d.   Both a and b are true.

24. For Althusser and Balibar, noncapitalist modes of production
a.   are stumbling blocks in the way of economic growth.
b.   are doomed to be overtaken by capitalism.
* c.   are often able to hold their own against encroaching capitalism.
d.   will be found in the periphery of the world system.

25. Since the collapse of communism in eastern Europe, what trends have come to characterize anthropological views of the political economy?
a.   Marxian theorists in many so-called "underdeveloped" societies have surged forward with the support of local groups behind them.
b.   Attention has been focused on social movements in so-called "underdeveloped societies," including vigilante movements, squatter movements in cities, movements defending the rights of women and homosexuals, and movements defending the rain forests.
c.   Anthropologists have studied the way ordinary citizens in many so-called "underdeveloped" societies have been trying to avoid both traditional capitalist and traditional marxian solutions for their problems.
* d.   Both b and c are true.

26. According to Arturo Escobar, the "new social movements" in Latin America are
a.   struggles over material conditions.
b.   struggles over meanings.
c.   attempts by people who have been marginalized in the "development" schemes of outsiders to build alternative forms of modern life.
* d.   all of the above

27. Beidelman argues that the whole reason for existence of religious missionizing is
a.   to enlighten people living in savagery.
b.   to make it easier for colonial powers to impose their rule.
c.   to spread modern medicine and education.
* d.   the undermining of a traditional way of life.

28. According to Beidelman, CMS missionaries saw their role in eastern Africa as one of wresting control of the region from
   a.   the Kaguru kings.
* b.   the Arabs.
   c.   the Germans.
   d.   the Catholic Church.

29. Perhaps the greatest irony revealed by Beidelman's study is that
   a.   the Kaguru converted to Catholicism as soon as the CMS missionaries were expelled from the country.
   b.   after independence, missionaries discovered that the Kaguru had been practicing their traditional rituals all along, in secret.
* c.   Kaguru who have rejected the CMS way of life are being asked by their own national government to live in much the same way.
   d.   after independence, increasing numbers of Kaguru converted to Islam.

30. According to Beidelman, CMS missionaries supported revivalism and yet were wary of participating fully in revivals with Africans because
   a.   they suspected that the Africans were actually practicing witchcraft when they said they were participating in revivals.
   b.   to get involved in revivals with Africans played into the hands of the colonial authorities.
   c.   participation in revivals with Africans diminished the prestige of CMS missionaries in the eyes of their Catholic competitors.
* d.   participation in revivals with Africans damaged their prestige and authority over their African converts.

31. Which of the following is an example of secular persuasion?
   a.   training peasants to use tractors
   b.   introducing a new strain of rice to local farmers
   c.   encouraging the production of cash crop sugar cane
* d.   all of the above

32. Lynn Morgan's study of health policy initiatives applied to Costa Rica in the 1970s by the United States Agency for International Development showed that
* a.   "popular participation" did not involve participation by the rural people for whom it was intended.
   b.   "popular participation" was successfully implemented as a mechanism for empowering rural communities.
   c.   "popular participation" was successful in stimulating democracy as the path to social equity.
   d.   Both b and c are true.

33. Gudeman's research in Panama allowed him to watch as his informants were transformed into

a.   self-sufficient peasants.

* b.   a rural labor force at the bottom of the capitalist order in Panama.

c.   prosperous ranchers with large herds of cattle.

d.   none of the above

34. Gudeman attributes the demise of the traditional economy in Los Boquerones to

a.   irreversible ecological factors over which the residents had no control.

b.   sound management practices which the peasants learned from development experts.

* c.   a prior distribution of resources meaning that landowners, not peasants, would control any profit-making ventures involving the land.

d.   the reworking of traditional kinship relations to meet the challenge of a world market in sugar cane.

35. Which of the following, according to Gudeman, characterizes the way peasants in Los Boquerones thought about rice and sugar cane?

a.   Rice had utility only when the peasant rid himself of it, the reverse of what he did with sugarcane.

* b.   Sugarcane had utility only when the peasant rid himself of it, the reverse of what he did with rice.

c.   Neither rice nor sugar cane had a role in the traditional peasant economy of Los Boquerones.

d.   Peasants regretted having to give up sugar cane farming to raise rice for the world market.

36. Luo-speakers of western Kenya who need land for production

a.   must buy it on the market or rent it.

b.   are forced to migrate out of their traditional homeland.

c.   can buy it, rent it, or ask their kin for a plot to use for cultivation.

d.   have engaged in warfare with their closest neighbors in recent years to obtain land.

37. The economic situation of the Luo-speakers of Kenya was described as an example of

a.   total capture of peasants by the capitalist market.

b.   articulating modes of production.

c.   the power of secular persuasion.

d.   the power of the gun.

38. According to Eric Wolf, the six major peasant wars of the twentieth century were waged in order to
    a. impose capitalism on a reluctant peasantry.
    b. impose communism on a reluctant peasantry.
*   c. to defend the way of life of middle peasants against the inroads of capitalism.
    d. export communism from Europe to the Third World.

39. According to Eric Wolf, the revolutionary change in social organization that developed during the Chinese and Vietnamese peasant revolutions was
    a. the imposition of alien socialist models on nonWestern societies.
*   b. the application of a communal village understanding of social organization to relations linking villages with one another and with the army.
    c. the successful imitation of the revolutionary example provided by the Russian revolution.
    d. the exclusion of soldiers and students from the peasant armies.

40. Anthropological studies of social, political, and economic change provide considerable evidence that
    a. human beings are passive in the face of the new.
*   b. human beings actively and resiliently respond to life's challenges.
    c. indigenous peoples are everywhere doomed to extinction in the face of the expansion of the capitalist world system.
    d. without the direction provided by theorists of social change from the "developed" world, ordinary citizens of "underdeveloped" lands cannot organize themselves in the face of diversity.

Essay Questions

41. The imposition of colonialism affected different groups in the colonized society in different ways. Discuss, illustrating with examples.

42. Dependency theorists argue that the inability of people in Third World countries to feed themselves is the direct outcome of the international capitalist economic order. On what grounds do they base this conclusion?

43. In capitalism, time is money. In subsistence agriculture, time is the surplus left people after they have produced enough food and seed for the next season. Discuss, illustrating with examples.

44. Why have some anthropologists found the concept of political economy to be useful in helping them understand the way societies in the Third World are structured? Discuss, giving examples.

45. What are the four major theoretical perspectives that anthropologists have used to try to explain the relationship between the West and the rest of the world? In what ways are they alike? On what points do they differ?

46. What is meant by sacred persuasion and secular persuasion in the context of social change in the nonWestern world? Give examples to illustrate your answer.

47. Is it inevitable that sooner or later all people everywhere will be captured by the capitalist market? Give examples to support your answer.

CHAPTER 24

ANTHROPOLOGY IN EVERYDAY LIFE

Outline

ANTHROPOLOGY BEYOND THE UNIVERSITY

Sorghum and Millet in Honduras and the Sudan
Lead Poisoning among Mexican-American Children
Anthropology and Policy
Anthropology and Human Rights

UNCERTAINTY AND AWARENESS

FREEDOM AND CONSTRAINT

Arguing Anthropology

1. Should anthropologist get involved in international development projects?

2. Why should people study anthropology?

Multiple Choice Questions

1. In the late twentieth century, applied anthropology became increasingly popular and important as a result of
a.   maturation of the discipline.
b.   the growing sophistication and awareness of the people with whom anthropologists have traditionally worked.
c.   a growing concern about how an anthropological approach could help solve problems in the anthropologists' own society.
*   d.   all of the above

2. In the late nineteenth century, when anthropology was first developing as a discipline, E. B. Tylor suggested that
a.   anthropology ought to concern itself with pure research.
*   b.   anthropology was a reformer's science.
c.   that the insights of professional anthropologists could not be appreciated by nonspecialists.
d.   both a and c

3. When anthropologists began to work for INTSORMIL in the mid-1970s, their goal was
   a. to get limited-resource farmers to plant newly developed strains of sorgum and millet.
   b. to find a way to convince limited-resource farmers to concentrate on crop production and give up raising livestock.
* c. to determine the techniques used by farmers with limited resources to cope with the social, economic, and ecological conditions under which they live.
   d. to get limited-resource farmers to appreciate how their traditional farming techniques were destroying the ecosystem.

4. As the INTSORMIL project progressed, the anthropologists found themselves
   a. having to demonstrate repeatedly the value of new crop strains to an uninterested audience of farmers.
* b. having to learn the languages and the conceptual systems of both the farmers and the agricultural scientists who were developing new strains of sorghum and millet.
   c. growing new crops in their own experiment station in order to demonstrate their value to reluctant farmers.
   d. teaching agricultural scientists participant-observation techniques as these scientists attempted to cultivate their new crops using traditional farming methods.

5. The anthropologists working on the INTSORMIL project discovered that the most significant constraints the farmers faced were
   a. uncertain rainfall and low soil fertility.
   b. inadequate labor and financial resources.
   c. the social and cultural systems in which the farmers were embedded.
* d. all of the above

6. As a result of the applied anthropologists' work, INTSORMIL learned
   a. the most effective way to break down traditional cultural barriers to new agricultural techniques.
   b. that small farmers in Honduras and Sudan were pretty much alike.
* c. that limited-resource farmers are not all alike.
   d. that limited-resource farmers with small herds of cattle were the most resistant to new ideas about farming.

7. The INTSORMIL staff was so impressed by the work of the applied anthropologists that it began to fund research aimed at
    a.   discovering how best to coordinate the laboratory duties of agricultural scientists with periods of fieldwork.
    b.   eliminating stock raising by limited-resource farmers by the year 2000.
* c.   modifying the existing varieties of sorghum to produce a better yielding local variety that can be grown together with other crops.
    d.   both b and c

8. When a Mexican-American child was treated for lead poisoning in the emergency room of a Los Angeles hospital in the summer of 1981, doctors discovered that
    a.   the child had been eating paint chips.
    b.   the heavy lead content in the air in the child's neighborhood was responsible.
* c.   the child had been given a folk remedy consisting of more than 90 percent elemental lead.
    d.   the child's family had been eating off pottery with an improperly treated lead glaze.

9. Dr. Robert Trotter was contacted by the Public Health Service in Dallas to investigate lead poisoning among Mexican-American children because
    a.   he was a specialist in environmental pollution who could help them devise a plan for cleaning up the air in Mexican-American neighborhoods near a local smelter.
* b.   he had done research on Mexican-American medicine.
    c.   he was an archaeologist with a vast knowledge of Mexican-American pottery types and could tell Mexican-Americans in Dallas how to treat their pottery to avoid lead poisoning in the future.
    d.   he had previously been successful in convincing Asian-Americans to switch from lead-based to latex-based paints when their children had been diagnosed with lead poisoning.

10. A task force in Colorado and California hired Trotter to create and implement a health education project that would
    a.   convince Mexican-Americans that their folk medical system was nonsense, and that only Western medicine could protect their children.
    b.   convince Mexican-Americans to switch from using pottery to using plastic dishes.
* c.   convince Mexican-Americans to switch from the lead-based remedy to another remedy that was already a part of their folk medical system, but which had no toxic side effects.
    d.   organize residents of Mexican-American neighborhoods to put pressure on smelter owners to clean up toxic emissions.

11. From Trotter's perspective, perhaps the most important overall result of his lead-poisoning research was
a. an increased awareness of the dangers of lead emissions from smelters among Mexican-Americans.
b. an increased awareness of the utility of anthropology in solving culturally related health care problems.
c. a government ban on the manufacture or importing of pottery with improperly treated lead glaze.
d. the fact that two years after the project began, lead-based paint was hard to find in the United States.

12. Cultural Survival is an anthropological organization concerned with
a. preserving traditional agricultural techniques in the face of pressures to modernize.
b. collecting and preserving the artwork of indigenous peoples whose societies have been destroyed by Westernization.
c. helping indigenous people and ethnic minorities deal as equals in their encounters with industrial society.
d. promoting the integration of indigenous healing practices and Western medicine.

13. Biological anthropologist Clyde Snow is best known for
a. his successful work of integrating indigenous healing practices and Western medicine in Mozambique following the 16-year civil war in that country.
b. having developed a new strain of sorghum better adapted to the Sudanese environment than indigenous strains.
c. training a team of Argentine medical and anthropology students to identify human remains and determine the causes of death of victims of the "dirty war" waged in Argentina in the 1970s.
d. improving yields for Honduran farmers by helping them figure out how to combine farming and herding.

14. The authors of this textbook believe that
a. knowing and experiencing cultural variety gives rise to doubt.
b. familiarity with alternative ways of living makes the ultimate meaning of any action a highly ambiguous matter.
c. ambiguity is part and parcel of the human condition.
d. all of the above

15. The authors of this textbook believe that
a. anthropological understanding can liberate the mind.
b. anthropological understanding can enrich human life.
c. anthropological understanding can help everyone imagine alternative ways of making it through the mine field of life.
* d. all of the above

Essay Questions

16. How do you think anthropology can help you in your major? In your chosen career? Defend your answer with examples.

17. Describe the history of applied anthropology in America. What have been the major changes in the way this subfield of anthropology has been viewed?

18. More than anything else, anthropology is a way of looking at the world. Discuss.

19. How would you explain cultural anthropology to a friend?